SpringerBriefs in Sociology

Series editor

Robert J. Johnson, Coral Gables, USA

For further volumes:
http://www.springer.com/series/10410

Zakir Husain · Mousumi Dutta

Women in Kolkata's IT Sector

Satisficing Between Work and Household

 Springer

Zakir Husain
Department of Humanities and
  Social Sciences
Indian Institute of Technology Kharagpur
Kharagpur, West Bengal
India

Mousumi Dutta
Department of Economics
Presidency University
Kolkata
India

ISSN 2212-6368
ISBN 978-81-322-1592-9
DOI 10.1007/978-81-322-1593-6
Springer New Delhi Heidelberg New York Dordrecht London

ISSN 2212-6376   (electronic)
ISBN 978-81-322-1593-6   (eBook)

Library of Congress Control Number: 2013956422

© The Author(s) 2014
This work is subject to copyright. All rights are reserved by the Publisher, whether the whole or part of the material is concerned, specifically the rights of translation, reprinting, reuse of illustrations, recitation, broadcasting, reproduction on microfilms or in any other physical way, and transmission or information storage and retrieval, electronic adaptation, computer software, or by similar or dissimilar methodology now known or hereafter developed. Exempted from this legal reservation are brief excerpts in connection with reviews or scholarly analysis or material supplied specifically for the purpose of being entered and executed on a computer system, for exclusive use by the purchaser of the work. Duplication of this publication or parts thereof is permitted only under the provisions of the Copyright Law of the Publisher's location, in its current version, and permission for use must always be obtained from Springer. Permissions for use may be obtained through RightsLink at the Copyright Clearance Center. Violations are liable to prosecution under the respective Copyright Law. The use of general descriptive names, registered names, trademarks, service marks, etc. in this publication does not imply, even in the absence of a specific statement, that such names are exempt from the relevant protective laws and regulations and therefore free for general use.
While the advice and information in this book are believed to be true and accurate at the date of publication, neither the authors nor the editors nor the publisher can accept any legal responsibility for any errors or omissions that may be made. The publisher makes no warranty, express or implied, with respect to the material contained herein.

Printed on acid-free paper

Springer is part of Springer Science+Business Media (www.springer.com)

To all the women who influenced us

To all the women who inspired us

Acknowledgments

This book is the output of a long study, starting in 2008 and culminating in 2013. During this time period many people aided our attempt to study the status of women workers in the IT sector.

The study is partly based on the output of a research project "Women, Work and Education", undertaken by the Institute of Development Studies Kolkata (IDSK), India, and funded by Rosa Luxemborg Society (Berlin, Germany). We wish to thank the funding agency for their generous assistance and to IDSK for providing the necessary infrastructural and administrative support to undertake the study. In particular we wish to thank Prof. Amiya Bagchi, Dr. Ramkrishna Chatterjee and Prof. Achin Chakraborty for their encouragement and support. We thank our Research Assistants, Sangeeta Dutta and Sanchita Mukherjee, for their hard and sincere efforts on the field, and during the process of data cleaning, editing, entry and analysis and Mr. Surit Das for his painstaking copy editing.

Initial findings were presented at three seminars—Annual Conference of The Indian Association of Labour Economics, Lucknow, India, 13–15 December 2008; Conference on International Competitiveness and Inclusive Development, organized by United Nations Conference on Trade And Development (UNCTAD) and Centre for Development Studies, Trivandrum, India, 20–21 October 2008; and Conference on Women, Work and Education, organized by IDSK, 22–23 August 2008. We are grateful to participants for their comments and suggestions that have helped to improve our work.

We received valuable comments from Prof. Bina Agrawal, Institute of Economic Growth, New Delhi, India. She suggested several useful papers that not only added breadth to the study, but also enabled us to situate the research problem in a historical framework. Anonymous reviewers also provided incisive comments and suggestions that greatly sharpened the thrust of the work. Any remaining errors remain our responsibility.

Finally, we wish to thank the respondents of the main survey undertaken in 2008 and the follow-up survey in 2013, for their patient responses to our probing, and those who facilitated the interviews.

Contents

Figures

Tables

Tables

Chapter 1
Women, Work and Agency: An Introduction

Abstract This chapter sets the tone of the book by laying out its conceptual framework, the context of the study and the issue to be examined. It defines empowerment, examines different empirical approaches to measure empowerment—particularly Amartya Sen's capability approach—and contrasts empowerment with agency. The methodology of the study and sample profile is also described.

Keywords Empowerment · Agency · Capability

1.1 Introduction

Since the 1980s the Indian economy and society has been involved in an irrevocable march towards globalisation and global interconnectedness. This process intensified in the 1990s, leading to a 'fundamental reordering of time and space' (Inda and Rosaldo 2002, p. 5). The global world, Inda and Rosaldo continue, is 'a world of motion, of complex interconnectedness.... (where) people readily ... cut across national boundaries, turning countless territories into spaces where various cultures converge, clash and struggle with each other, ... providing people with resources from which to fashion new ways of being in the world' (2002, pp. 3–4). These processes are perhaps most stamped in the Information Technology (IT) industry.

IT is concerned with the development, management and use of computer-based information systems. A typical IT firm would be responsible for storing information, protecting information, processing the information, transmitting the information as necessary and later retrieving information as necessary. While mankind has been storing, retrieving, manipulating and communicating information since prehistoric times, major innovations leading to the emergence of the IT industry—development of integrated circuits, operating systems, central processing units, personal computers, World Wide Web, database management systems and other innovations—occurred mainly after the Second World War. In 1958, observing these developments Leavitt and Whisler commented:

Z. Husain and M. Dutta, *Women in Kolkata's IT Sector*,
SpringerBriefs in Sociology, DOI: 10.1007/978-81-322-1593-6_1,
© The Author(s) 2014

> Over the last decade a new technology has begun to take hold in American business, one so new that its significance is still difficult to evaluate. While many aspects of this technology are uncertain, it seems clear that it will move into the managerial scene rapidly, with definite and far-reaching impact on managerial organisation. ... The new technology does not yet have a single established name. We shall call it Information Technology (Leavitt and Whisler 1958, p. 1).

Although IT includes hardware as well, we will restrict our attention to the following segments of the industry:

(a) Software development: Software development refers to all activities ranging from the conception of the desired software to the final manifestation of the software, ideally in a planned and structured process.
(b) Business Process Outsourcing (BPO): Business Process Outsourcing refers to the transmission of processes along with the associated operational activities and responsibilities to a third party with at least a guaranteed equal service level.
(c) Knowledge Processing Outsourcing activities (KPO): Knowledge Process Outsourcing is a form of outsourcing in which knowledge- or information-related work is carried out by workers in a different company in the same country or on an offshore location to save cost. This typically involves high-value work carried out by highly skilled staff.
(d) Call Centres: A call centre is a centralised office used for the purpose of receiving and transmitting a large volume of requests by telephone. It is operated by a company to administer incoming product support or information enquiries by consumers. Outgoing calls for telemarketing, clientele and debt collection are also made.

The latter three constitute what is known as the Information Technology Enabled Services (ITES). This is defined as outsourcing of processes that can be enabled with Information Technology and covers diverse areas like finance, human relations, administration, health care, telecommunication, travel and tourism, etc.

The IT industry has been a driving force underlying globalisation. Techno-logical innovations in computer hardware, software and telecommunications greatly increased ability to access information in the 1990s. This had a multiplier effect on the economy. Simultaneously, advancements in Internet-based tools over the past 5–10 years, such as social networking websites, twitter and other Web-based applications are changing the way people use and share information for personal, political and commercial purposes. These developments have increased efficiency in all sectors of the economy. Most important, IT diverts resources in new channels, promoting new products and ideas across nations and cultures, regardless of geographical location. Creating efficient and effective channels for the exchange of information, IT has been the catalyst for global integration on an unmarked scale, rendering irrelevant geographic and political boundaries and enabling freer flow of culture and information across boundaries.

1.2 Women in IT Sector

The IT revolution has witnessed the emergence of demand for a highly skilled labour force that may be located at a physical distance from the client. This has resulted in the location of IT companies in developing countries with cheap labour and heavily subsidised education sector. The rapidly increasing labour demand has led to the recruitment of women workers in the IT industry on a scale that is large in absolute, if not relative, terms. Fuller and Narasimhan (2007) estimated that in 2005 there were over one million IT workers in India. In the software sector, where about a third of these IT professionals work, one out of every four workers are women. In the IT Enabled Services (ITES) and Business Processing Outsourcing (BPO) sectors, where the work is less technical and more routine, employers prefer women workers. This is because employers perceive women to be docile, hard-working and sincere workers, who are also less likely to unionise. In such sectors, women workers outnumber men by two is to one ratio (NASSCOM 2003). Almost all the workers are young, urban residents and at least graduates. Their high pay (by Indian standards)—before restrictions on outsourcing in USA cut down jobs in the industry—made them an important part of the Indian emerging middle class.

Given the link between work, economic independence and agency—theorised in the vast literature on gender and development—one would expect that the rapid changes within society and the consequent flux would throw up opportunities for women to break down patriarchal barriers on their choices and agency and move to a higher level of empowerment. In particular, such opportunities are anticipated in high growth sectors like the IT industry. This work examines whether this has happened in reality. In particular, we examine whether women workers in the IT sector have been able to shed restrictions on their agency imposed by a patriarchal Indian society, or whether the cocktail of globalisation and patriarchy has imposed new burdens on these women. To answer this question we must first understand what is agency and empowerment. This will help us to define the parameters by which the impact of the growth of the IT sector in the context of a globalising world may be evaluated.

1.3 Empowerment and Agency

The importance of women's empowerment in the developmental process has been reiterated in discourses undertaken in recent United Nations (UN) conferences. For instance, the United Nations Conference on Environment and Development (UNCED) Agenda 21 (1992) mentions women's advancement and empowerment in decision-making, including women's participation in 'national and international ecosystem management and control of environment degradation' as a key area for sustainable development. The importance of women's empowerment in demography was underlined in the International Conference on Population and

Development (ICPD) in Cairo, 1994. The Conference stressed that women should be empowered to take informed choices with respect to their health and reproductive outcomes. The 1995 Copenhagen Declaration of the World Summit on Social Development (WSSD) argued that empowering people, particularly women, to strengthen functional capacities is a major objective of development. The participatory nature of the process of empowerment was recognised in the Copenhagen Declaration and in the Report of the UN Fourth World Conference on Women called its Platform for Action an agenda for women's empowerment, meaning that the principle of shared power and responsibility should be established between women and men at home, in the workplace and in the wider national and international communities (UN 1995).

Despite the widespread usage of the term 'empowerment' and recognition of its importance, it is generally not defined by the users. The next section, therefore, briefly discusses some important definitions of empowerment.

1.3.1 Towards an Understanding of Empowerment

The Human Development Report (UNDP 1995) focuses on the participatory aspect of empowerment:

> Development must be *by* people, not only *for* them. People must participate fully in the decisions and processes that shape their lives… but at the same time this promotes a rather instrumentalist view of empowerment; investing in women's capabilities and empowering them to exercise their choices is not only valuable in itself but is also the surest way to contribute to economic growth and overall development (UNDP 1995).

Another view stresses empowerment as freedom from oppression and inequality:

> Empowerment involves challenging the forms of oppression which compel millions of people to play a part in their society on terms which are inequitable, or in ways which deny their human rights (Oxfam 1995).

Feminist activists stress that empowerment of women is not about replacing one form of empowerment with another:

> Women's empowerment should lead to the liberation of men from false value systems and ideologies of oppression. It should lead to a situation where each one can become a whole being regardless of gender, and use their fullest potential to construct a more humane society for all (Akhtar and UBINIG 1992, personal communication quoted in Batliwala 1994, p. 131).

Development Alternatives for Women in New Era, a Southern network of researchers, policy makers and activists also underlines this point:

> The women's movement … at its deepest it is not an effort to play 'catch-up' with the competitive, aggressive 'dog-eat-dog' spirit of the dominant system. It is rather, an attempt to convert men and the system to the sense of responsibility, nurturance, openness and rejection of hierarchy that are part of our vision (Sen and Grown 1985, p. 72).

Oxaal and Baden (1997) argue that the idea of power is at the root of the term empowerment. While power can be understood as operating in a number of different ways—power over,[1] power to,[2] power with[3] and power within[4]—the feminist movement has emphasised collective organisation ('power with') and has been influential in developing ideas about 'power within'. Shifting from the initial aggressive approach, seeking to challenge power structures that marginalize women, activists now tend to seek ways to increase self-confidence and self-reliance.

As Mayoux (1998) suggests, for instance, empowerment is a process of internal change, augmentation of capabilities and collective mobilisation of women for the questioning and changing of the subordination connected with gender. Or, as Deepa Narayan defines empowerment, 'Empowerment is the expansion of freedom of choice and action. It means increasing one's authority and control over the resources and decisions that affects one's life' (Narayan 2005, p. 14).

1.3.2 Macro Measures

The Human Development Report (UNDP 1995) states empowerment as one of the four essential components of the human development paradigm, the others being productivity, equity and sustainability. Empowerment is described as people fully participating in the decisions and processes that shape their lives. The UNDP's Human Development Report of 1995 introduced two new complementary indices: the Gender-related Development Index (GDI) and the Gender Empowerment Measure (GEM). The GDI indicator measures the inequalities between men and women in terms of access to basic needs. On the other hand, GEM evaluates women's access to political and economic posts. The three indicators used are the share of seats held by women in the parliamentary assemblies, the share of supervisory posts, high administrative posts and technical posts assumed by women, and the estimated share of income from work of women compared to that of men. It aims to examine whether women and men are able to actively participate in economic and political life and take part in decision-making.

---

[1] This power involves an either/or relationship of domination/subordination. Ultimately, it is based on socially sanctioned threats of violence and intimidation, it requires constant vigilance to maintain, and it invites active and passive resistance.

[2] This power relates to having decision-making authority, power to solve problems and can be creative and enabling.

[3] This power involves people organising with a common purpose or common understanding to achieve collective goals.

[4] This power refers to self confidence, self awareness and assertiveness. It relates to how can individuals can recognise through analysing their experience how power operates in their lives, and gain the confidence to act to influence and change this (Williams et al. 1994).

Based on Amartya Sen's work (1984, 1985, 1990a), UNDP makes the distinction between the measure of inequality and empowerment. While the GDI focuses on the extension of capabilities the GEM is concerned with the use of those capabilities to take advantage of the opportunities of life.

Swain (2006) identifies some limitations of these indices. First, they focus on quantitative aspects, without considering whether they reflect the reality or not. For instance, the presence of a large proportion of elected women members in the national parliament does not necessarily have significant real power. Secondly, such a measure does not take into account the participation of women in the local political institutions and their visibility in other bodies of civil society. A third limitation of the macro approach is that it focuses on countries. But, it is also necessary to study and estimate the inter-person disparities *within* a country. This approach is based on Sen's capability approach, and it is necessary to understand this approach before proceeding to examine how micro-measures of gender disparity and empowerment can be developed.

1.3.3 Sen's Capability Approach

Sen begins by considering income. This indicates the ability to command or possess commodities. Sen (1983) accepts the position adopted by the classical philosopher, Adam Smith, that economic growth and the expansion in the set of commodities and services available to the population is necessary for human development. However, he argues that commodities are not important for themselves, but as resources. That is they are instruments or means to attain some other things (Sen 1990a). What is important, according to Sen, is what people are able to achieve, and it is at this level that another important form of disparity may emerge (apart from differences in endowments of commodities). Sen points out that different people and different societies may differ in their capacity to convert income and commodities (resources) into valuable achievements. There may be several reasons for this—personal, social, cultural and other environmental reasons. For instance, a woman with the same commodity vector as a man may be unable to undertake the same actions due to cultural restrictions. Looking merely at the commodity bundle possessed by a person, therefore, is inadequate as it does not indicate how well people can *function* with the goods and services available to them.

Apparently, the utility-based welfare approach can overcome this deficiency as it focuses on the level of satisfaction that a person can achieve. But, Sen (1984) points out, utility does not distinguish between different sources of pleasure or pain or different kinds of desires. For instance, utility fails to discriminate against offensive tastes. More important, there is more to life than simply pleasure or utility (Sen 1984). There are many things of intrinsic value, like rights and positive freedoms, neglected by the welfare approach. In particular, utility experienced by a person may be influenced by socio-cultural forces that increase/decrease expectations of the person. For instance, Sen (1985) found that there were significant differences between externally observed health of widows and their own subjective impressions of their physical state.

Sen concludes that neither command over resources nor utility presents an adequate measure of human well-being or deprivation. A more direct approach is required, concentrating on *functionings* and *capabilities*. Functionings refer to beings and doings, or achievements and outcomes. Examples are being well fed, sheltered, getting education and so on. Capabilities, on the other hand, are *potential* functionings—they refer to opportunities or freedom to achieve something. All capabilities jointly define the overall freedom that a person enjoys to lead the life he/she values.[5]

Strictly speaking, the capability approach is not a theory but a framework (Robeyns 2003). This imparts the approach with a flexibility that allows researchers to expand the approach in different directions. For instance, Sen has claimed that his approach is relevant to studying gender disparities and feminist issues:

> ... the question of gender inequality ... can be understood much better by comparing those things that intrinsically matter (such as functionings and capabilities), rather than just the means like ... resources. The issue of gender inequality is ultimately one of disparate freedoms (Sen 1992, p. 125).

1.3.4 Micro-Based Measures

The capability approach allows researchers in the field of gender to highlight important issues like reproductive health, voting rights, political power, domestic violence, education and women's social status. But, there is one barrier to such application. Robeyns (2003) argues that Sen has not identified which capabilities are relevant if we want to assess disparities. What researchers require is a well-defined list of capabilities.

While Nussbaum also stresses the need for a specific list of 'central human capabilities' (Nussbaum 1990, 1995, 2000), Robeyns (2003) departs from Nussbaum by arguing that the under specified nature of Sen's approach calls for context- and application-specific lists of capabilities. Such lists will vary from one geographical region to another, and between (say) applications in the field of health to applications in the field of gender.[6]

---

[5] An example illustrates the difference between functioning and capabilities. Compare two persons who are fasting. One of them is a poor Indian farmer, conditioned by years of hardship to expect little from life. Another is a protestor in a developed country. While the outcome or functionings (level of nutrition) of both persons are the same, they differ substantially in their capabilities to escape from the current outcome.

[6] Sen himself refuses to tie himself to any central list and argues that such lists are entirely context specific and must be defined through a participative process (Sen 1999, 2004).

Robeyns (2003) proceeds to develop a list of capabilities to conceptualise gender inequality:

1. Life and physical health
2. Mental well-being
3. Bodily integrity
4. Social relations
5. Political empowerment
6. Education and knowledge
7. Social reproduction and non-market care
8. Paid work and other projects
9. Shelter and environment
10. Mobility
11. Leisure activities
12. Time autonomy
13. Respect
14. Religion and spirituality

Sugden (1993) has questioned how far Sen's approach is operational. This point has been reiterated by other scholars (Ysander 1993; Srinivasan 1994; Roemer 1996). The lack of a list of capabilities is the main reason underlying this sceptism (Williams 1987; Nussbaum 1988; Qizilbash 1998). In response, researchers have developed their own lists of capabilities central to their enquiry and tried to identify either determinants of outcomes or attempt inter-personal comparison of outcomes—particularly in the field of gender studies—using a variety of statistical methods, like fuzzy sets theory (Lelli 2001; Martinetti 2000; Qizilbash 2002), factor analysis (Schokkaert and Van Ootegem 1990; Balestrino and Sciclone 2000; Lelli 2001; Klassen 2000; Maasoumi and Nickelsburg 1988), time series clustering (Mcgee and Carlton 1970; Piccolo 1970; Hobijn and Frances 2000; Hirschbeerg et al. 2001), regression models (Martinetti 2000; Klassen 2000; Lelli 2001; Schokkaert and Van Ootegem 1990) and Structural Equation Model (Raiser et al. 2000; Chakrabarti and Sharma Biswas 2008; Bhattacharya 2008). Kuklys provides a useful summary of such methods (Kuklys 2005, pp. 31–44).

1.3.5 Agency

Agency and empowerment have sometimes been used interchangeably. Alkire, for instance, sometimes switches from one to the other in mid-sentence, on one occasion noting that they are 'related but often differently defined' (Alkire 2008, p. 2). Nevertheless, there are intrinsic differences between the two.

We had previously seen that 'people are empowered insofar as they become better able to shape their own lives' (Narayan 2005, p. 4). This implies that empowerment presupposes a process of change to produce a better outcome. So 'empowerment' evidently refers not to a state of affairs but to a process of change with a specific kind of result. In this respect it differs from 'agency,' which refers 'either to a given person's degree of involvement in a course of action, or to the scope of actions that a person could be involved in bringing about' (Drydyk 2008a, p. 3). In other words, 'agency' refers to a state of affairs while 'empowerment' refers to a process of change.

Drydyk continues:

> Sen first introduced an idea of agency as an evaluative space contrasting with capability. The valuable functionings that a person has reason to value, and actually manages to achieve, comprise that person's wellbeing achievement. The alternative combinations of functionings that a person can achieve comprise that person's capability, or wellbeing freedom. The property of increasing a person's wellbeing freedom is a good-making property: for instance, what makes some drugs good or advantageous is that they can be used to expand our wellbeing freedom, specifically by enabling us to stay healthy, or indeed to stay alive. Agency, by contrast, is conceived in terms of achieving goals that people happen to value, rather than functioning in ways that they have reason to value. Such goals may be other-regarding or in other ways unrelated to the person's own wellbeing. This too is a source of advantage or disadvantage, defining an evaluative space. So some drugs may also be advantageous to athletes by enabling them to win competitions, even if some health risks are involved. 'Agency' in this sense refers to a person's scope for achieving that person's valued goals.
>
> The role of 'agency' in this sense, within the capability approach, has been to supplement wellbeing freedom as an evaluative space exhibiting the inequalities that should matter for social policy and social justice. It was thought to be a necessary supplement because the important inequalities may not just be about individuals' own wellbeing; people have other causes and concerns, some altruistic, and unequal freedom to successfully pursue these causes and concerns can also be a significant inequality (Drydyk 2008a, pp. 3–4).

Crocker and Robeyns (2008) argue that some people are more involved in their actions than others—they display a greater degree of agency in their actions than others, or even what they normally do at other times.[7] The degree to which agency is exercised depends upon (a) a person either performs an activity or plays a role in performing it, (b) this activity has an impact on the world, (c) the activity was chosen by the person or imposed by outside (d) for reasons of their own (in individual or group deliberation). The last two points are of particular importance in our study on understanding the relationship between agency and empowerment.

Consider a situation when women are attempting to make a choice. Their conception of a good choice cannot be formed in vacuum, but is socially and culturally defined. If these norms are not empowering, then agency (or involvement) does not empower the actors. For instance,

> The need to bear the approved number of children in order to secure social status and family approval takes its toll on women's bodies and on their lives as they bear children beyond their capacity. Furthermore, status considerations in cultures of son-preference require women to give birth to a certain number of sons; to favour their sons over their daughters in ways that reinforce social discrimination against women; and to bring their

---

[7] Crocker and Robeyns (2008) Capability and Agency. Draft manuscript, 18 January, cited by Drydyk (2008b, p. 4).

daughters up to devalue themselves, thereby acting as agents in the transmission of gender discrimination over generations. (Kabeer 1999, p. 40)

This generates a dilemma for empowerment (Drydyk 2008b). This dilemma can be solved if we consider whether the norms are imposed upon by outside and internalised, or derived (or chosen) from within through a conscious process of choice. Although the process of deliberation or choice occurs in a social context, the agency exercised in choosing the norm separates it from norms blindly chosen by the actors.

> The notion of agency attributes to the individual actor the capacity to process social experience and to devise ways of coping with life eve under conditions of extreme coercion. Within the limits of information, uncertainty and other constraints that exist, social actor are 'knowledgeable' and 'capable'. ...As social actors, (women) face alternative ways of formulating their objectives, however restricted their resources (Moser and Clark 2001, p. 5).

Women with poor endowments, for instance, may choose to follow a patriarchal norm so as not to disturb her marital life and affect her long run well-being. Nevertheless, such women have at least progressed further on the road to empowerment than women who blindly internalise such norms. The difference between the two is that, given windows of opportunity, the former may attempt to adopt strategies that help her to be less marginalised and more empowered. One such window is employment.

1.4 Employment, Capabilities and Empowerment

Empowerment levels are contingent upon a host of factors and their inter-relationships. In contrast, economic independence—attained through participation in economic activities—is often identified as a necessary, but not sufficient, condition for increasing capabilities, and hence empowerment (Braunstein 2008; World Bank 2012). The logic underlying this argument may be summarised in terms of a simple intra-household bargaining model (Sen 1990b; Agarwal 1994).

Sen (1990b) argues that households produce in a context of cooperation and conflict. On one hand, they combine the capacities of household members to produce a stream of goods and services as a collective household; on the other hand, the production decision and rules for distribution of output reflects the common but differing priorities of individual members. The outcome depends upon:

(a) one's alternatives to remaining in the household (exit option, or fall back position) and
(b) one's right or ability to try and influence household decisions (voice or autonomy), including decisions about one's own strategic life choices.

Agarwal (1994) argues that social norms and economic realities combine to create misperceptions about women's contribution to household activities (perceived contribution response) and their right to 'enjoy' a fair share of the household outcome (perceived interest response). This affects the fallback position adversely and also curtails women's autonomy. The result is an equilibrium solution biased against women.

Participation of women in economic activities has the potential to affect the equilibrium solution by ensuring that the women are economically independent. This improves their fallback position, so that they can use the exit option as a credible threat to force a more equitable solution of the intra-household bargaining model. Of course, this is only a potential effect. Studies on micro-credit have found that in many cases the credit provided to women are appropriated by their husbands or other male relatives (Zareen and Khan 2001; Goetz and Gupta 1996; Rahman 1998; Parvin et al. 2004). In the absence of control over income, the fallback position of women—and hence their bargaining power within the household—improves only marginally, so that they are unable to improve their status within the household domain substantially. Despite this, economic independence is recognised as a *necessary* condition for gender empowerment. Hence, a study of workforce participation of women and its implications is of considerable importance in understanding gender emancipation.

Global trends in participation of women in the labour market have not been encouraging (see Appendix Tables A.1 and A.2). An ILO (International Labour Organisation) report observes that

> despite the progress made in many regions, far fewer women participate in labour markets than men. In developed economies, part of the gender gaps in participation and employment can be attributed to the fact that some women freely choose to stay at home and can afford not to enter the labour market. Yet in some developing regions of the world, remaining outside of the labour force is not a choice for the majority of women but an obligation; it is likely that women would opt to work in these regions if it became socially acceptable to do so. This of course does not mean that these women remain at home doing nothing; most are heavily engaged in household activities and unpaid family care responsibilities. Regardless, because most female household work continues to be classified as non-economic activity, the women who are thus occupied are classified as outside of the labour force (ILO 2009, p. 10).

The ILO study also observes that gender inequalities remain a persistent feature of the labour market, particularly in developing countries:

> Women are also often in a disadvantaged position in terms of the share of vulnerable employment (i.e. unpaid family workers and own-account workers) in total employment. These workers are most likely to be characterised by insecure employment, low earnings and low productivity. Those women who are able to secure the relative comfort of wage and salaried employment are often not receiving the same remuneration as their male counterparts. Gender wage differentials may be due to a variety of factors, including crowding of women in low paying industries and differences in skills and work experience, but may also be the result of discrimination (ILO 2009, p. 6).

Overall, increasing participation of women in the labour market has belied expectations and failed to improve their status and sense of agency. This is partly because of the nature of engagement in economic activities. Now, in recent years, the influx of foreign capital has increased the demand for a technically skilled labour force substantially in certain sectors. The sharp increase in labour demand reduces the scope for gender discrimination in recruitment policy. Rather, a sense of corporate social responsibility and increasing media scrutiny has often led to conscious attempts to increase the proportion of women workers in these sectors (NASSCOM 2003; COD 2004). For instance, a MERCER-NASSCOM study found that in 2007–2008 employment of women in the IT sector had increased by 60 %, so that by the end of 2008 there were 6.7 million women working in the IT sector.[8] Given that these women workers are highly educated, earn very high wages and are often married to educated spouses from affluent families, it was expected that employment would enhance the empowerment levels of such workers (Clark and Sekher 2007; Shanker 2008). In reality, the cocktail of patriarchy and globalisation imposed a dual burden on the workers. On one hand, they were expected to compete on even terms with their male counterparts, while, on the other hand, they were expected to conform to the traditional image of women as provider of care services to spouse, children and in-laws at home (Mitter and Rowbotham 1995).

1.5 Research Objective

This study examines the status of women workers in the IT sector in Kolkata, a metropolitan city in eastern India. It seeks to examine the impact of employment in a highly skill-intensive sector characterised by a corporate environment on empowerment. Does it provide space to the women workers to balance work and household responsibilities satisfying the set of values held by the women workers? Or, does the synergy of global capitalism and local patriarchy create new bounds on the freedom of choice of women.

This study is another addition to the existing body of literature on the status of women workers in the IT sector. We argue that the book makes a contribution to the existing literature in two ways. First, studies of women workers in Kolkata's IT sector are rare, even though the city has emerged as an important IT hub in recent years. Second, this work attempts to make an intellectual departure from existing studies of women workers in India's IT sector. Contrary to the existing studies portraying women as disempowered agents burdened by the dual responsibility of work and household, this work takes a more positive stance towards the problem. We argue that in the post globalised world, decisions are increasingly becoming individualised, though influenced by the situational and historical context. In particular, patriarchal foundations of the Indian family are weakening, enabling women

---

[8] Reported in Economic Times (13 May 2009).

workers—at least from urban educated families—to break out of a passive mould and trying to carve out their own destiny. The decision-making model used is Simon's satisficing framework (Simon 1956). Simultaneously, we also borrow from the sociological literature on women's work and family—in particular, Cynthia Hakim's studies (Hakim 1991, 1995, 1996a, b)—and, of course, Sen's work on capabilities.

1.6 Methodology

The study is mainly based on a primary survey of women workers in Kolkata's IT sector. The survey was undertaken between July and October 2008. Initially, we approached IT companies and sought permission to interview some of the women workers. Unfortunately most companies refused access to women workers. Part of the reason is no doubt the negative image created by the public media about this sector. Only three companies permitted us to interview selected women workers on the condition of anonymity.

Consequently, we adopted the snowball sampling method. This method is also referred to as chain sampling, chain-referral sampling and referral sampling. It is a non-probability sampling technique where existing study subjects recruit future subjects from among their acquaintances (Goodman 1961). The name snowball sampling is used because as more relationships are built through mutual associ-ation, more connections can be made through those new relationships. This allows a plethora of information to be shared and collected. The sampling process resembles a snowball that rolls and increases in size as it collects more snow.

As the sample builds up, enough data are gathered to be useful for research. Snowball sampling is often used in situations when the target population is hidden or access to them restricted, making it difficult for researchers to locate them. Examples are surveys of drug users, sex workers, homosexuals and similar groups. Snowball sampling is a useful tool for building networks and increasing the number of participants. However, the success of this technique depends greatly on the initial contacts and connections made. Thus it is important to start the process with popular and reliable respondents. This will not only allow the sample to expand rapidly, but ensure credible and dependable information. Our survey used respondents from the companies that permitted us to interview their employees or those referred by colleagues, friends or relatives as anchoring points. These respondents were requested to refer us to other colleagues in the industry. In all, we managed to interview 114 respondents. Respondents were initially interviewed using a structured, mostly close-ended questionnaire.

Respondents were selected from different segments of the IT industry. Some of them were software engineers working in multinational corporations, or leading Indian companies; others were working in smaller Indian companies. We inter-viewed workers from call centres, medical transcriptions and other workers in the BPO and KPO sectors. The segment-wise break-up of the sample is given in Table 1.1.

Table 1.1 Composition of
sample by segment

Segment	Number	Percentage
Software development	37	32.5
Knowledge processing	25	21.9
Business processing	28	24.6
Call centres	17	14.9
Other ITES segments[a]	7	6.1
TOTAL	114	100

[a] Comprising Medical Transcription, Travel and Tourism, etc.

After undertaking the first-phase interview, we selected about 10 % of the respondents for detailed profiling. Respondents were interviewed either at home or in their office canteens for an hour. During this interview, we probed their family background, reasons for joining the IT sector, their work experience, aspirations, expectations of family, how they deal with pressure at home and work and similar issues. The issue of child care was also discussed. The respondents used illustrations from—their own experiences, and also that of their colleagues—during these interviews.

In 2013, we undertook a survey of four more respondents. Again detailed unstructured interviews were taken, exploring the issues examined earlier. In addition, we tried to see if there was any impact of the regulations on outsourcing introduced in 2009 by the Obama government on their agency and empowerment.

In addition to the primary data we also used unit level data from the National Sample Survey Organization (NSSO) quinquenniel surveys on 'Employment and Unemployment'. These surveys—providing reliable data on education and earnings of workers classified into occupational categories—are considered by researchers and policy makers to be one of the most reliable sample surveys in India. We have used data from the last two rounds or waves—the 61st round (2004–2005) and 66th round (2009–2010). This allows us to examine whether there has been any change in the extent of discrimination in the IT sector, particularly after the global recession.

After extracting the unit level data, we had to identify workers whose occupational codes matched with the IT and related sectors. Now occupation is given for three types of workers—principal status, subsidiary status and current weekly status. Principal status workers are those workers who have been employed for the major part of the year preceding the date of survey. In addition, some workers also have some side activity that they may have been performing for a large part of the year preceding the survey. Such workers are called subsidiary workers. Finally, respondents are asked whether they had worked in the week preceding the survey. This refers to the current weekly status. Normally, researchers focus on principal activity status. The logic is that this indicates what the person has mostly been doing over the last year. In contrast, current weekly status covers only one week. Data on earnings is obtained only for current weekly status. Hence we used weekly status. The use of weekly status, rather than principal status, does not affect the validity of our findings as there is unlikely to be difference between occupation

Table 1.2 Identification of IT sector workers using NCO codes

2004 code	Occupation
721	Hardware consultancy
722	Software consultancy and supply
723	Database processing and related activities
724, 725	Maintenance and repair of computing, office and accounting machinery
729	Other computer-related activities

Table 1.3 Distribution of workers by occupation, gender and round

Occupation	61st round			66th round		
	Male	Female	Total	Male	Female	Total
Hardware	9	1	10	32	6	38
Software	138	34	172	–	–	–
Data processing	32	12	44	61	16	77
Database related	19	6	25	20	2	22
Maintenance and repairing	25	0	25	45	3	48
Others	54	14	68	–	–	–
Total	227	67	344	158	27	185

Source Estimated from unit level data, 61st and 66th rounds

classified by weekly status and principal status in the formal sector. It is only in the informal economy where labour turnover rates and inter-occupational mobility are very high that there will be major differences in occupational classification by principal and weekly status.

Workers are classified into occupational categories using the National Classification of Occupation (NCO). The classification was first drawn up in 1968 and has been used by NSSO till the 61st round. The 64th round, in contrast, uses the revised NCO system of 2004. Using NSSO data, we selected workers with the following codes (Table 1.2). Data on this sub-sample were analysed to obtain their educational profile and daily earnings. The all-India sample was used as there were only a handful of respondents from West Bengal.

Information on other workers are deleted so that we have data on education, age, gender, weekly earnings, number of days worked and other socio-economic parameters. In the 61st round we have 344 workers belonging to the IT sector; in the 66th round, the number of workers in the IT sector surveyed decreases to 185. These workers may be further sub-divided by sex and occupation as follows (Table 1.3).

The NSSO data is used to test for disparity in earnings using univariate statistical methods. In addition a regression model was also estimated using the Ordinary Least Square method.

1.7 Chapter Scheme

The book is structured as follows: We start with a critical review of the Marxist literature on the impact of employment of women on export-based industries (Chap. 2). Works by Elson and Pearson (1981) and Banerjee (1991, 1992) have shown that mere integration of women in development is not enough, it is necessary to examine the process of this integration. A brief review of the studies of women workers in the IT sector follows. Such studies are pessimistic and show that the synergy of capitalism and patriarchy creates an environment inhibiting, rather than encouraging, women's agency. On the other hand, Lim (1990) has argued that the ideological base of this school led to a methodologically flawed approach over-looking key aspects of the status of women workers in export industries of South-east Asia and Mexico. Moreover, these works held a binary perspective, viewing men as active agents always exploiting women who are without any agency.

This binary perspective forms the starting point of our critique of Marxist literature in Chap. 3. We first identify the limitations of the Marxist school and then turn to an analysis of the feminist literature emerging from the late 1980s. This approach questions the view that the lack of overt resistance implies that women are passive agents exploited by a patriarchal society. It delves into the complexities of the binary victim–agent model to reveal the subtle ways in which women try to negotiate and re-negotiate their roles in society through a process of subversion and covert resistance (patriarchal bargaining). This view, we argue, offers a more promising approach to the problem of autonomy and agency. We then present an alternative framework based on the theory of sociologist, Cynthia Hakim and economist, Herbert Simon that will be used to analyse the findings of the survey.

In the next chapter we turn to the IT industry. We begin with a brief history of the evolution of this industry and its growth in India; we also identify the linkages of this sector with other parts of the economy to establish the importance of the IT industry in India. The emergence of Kolkata as an important IT hub in eastern India is described next. The findings of our analysis—based on NSSO data and data collected in our survey of women workers—conclude Chap. 4.

Chapter 5 uses the analytical framework developed in Chap. 3 to show that working in the IT industry has provided some much needed space and autonomy to the women workers. Although there are biases in the working environment, favourable historical trends and socio-economic context have reduced the intensity of the work–home conflict and enhanced autonomy of women. The concluding chapter summarises the main findings of the study.

References

Agarwal, B. (1994). *A field of one's own: Gender and land rights in South Asia*, Cambridge: New Delhi.

Alkire, S. (2008). *Concepts and measures of agency*. OPHI Working Paper Series, Working Paper No. 9. Oxford: Oxford Poverty and Human Development Initiative.

Balestrino, A., & Sciclone, N. (2000). *Should we use functionings instead of income to measure wellbeing? Theory, and some evidence from Italy*. Mimeo: University of Pisa.

Banerjee, N. (1991). *Indian women in a changing industrial scenario*. New Delhi: Sage Publishers.

Banerjee, N. (1992). *Poverty, work and gender in urban India*. Occasional Papers No. 133, Kolkata: Centre for Studies in Social Sciences.

Batliwala, S. (1994). The meaning of women's empowerment: New concepts from action. In G. Sen, A. Germain, & L. Chen (Eds.), *Population policies reconsidered, Havard series on population and international health*. Boston: Harvard University Press, 127–138.

Bhattacharya, J. (2008). *Self help groups and capability enhancements: A study in two selected districts of West Bengal. Mimeograph*. Siena, Italy: Department of Economia and Politica, Sienna University.

Braunstein, E. (2008). *Women's employment, empowerment and globalization: An economic perspective*. New York, United Nations: Division for the advancement of women, Department of Economic and Social Affairs.

Centre for Organization Development. (2004). *Final Report on Women in Information Technology*. Hyderabad: Report submitted to Department of Women and Child, Ministry of Human Resource Development, Government of India.

Chakrabarti, S., & Sharma Biswas, C. (2008). *Women empowerment, household condition and personal characteristics: Their interdependencies in developing countries. Discussion paper*. Kolkata: Economic Research Unit, Indian Statistical Institute.

Clarke, A., & Sekher, T. V. (2007). Can career-minded young women reverse gender discrimination? *A View from Bangalore's High Tech Sector, Gender, Technology and Development, 11*(3), 285–319.

Crocker, D., & Robeyns, I. (2008). Capability and Agency. Draft manuscript, 18 January.

Drydyk, J. (2008a). Durable empowerment. *Journal of Global Ethics, 4*(3), 231–245.

Drydyk, J. (2008b). *How to distinguish empowerment from agency?* Retrieved May 4 2013 from http://bit.ly/11oLTl4

Elson, D., & Pearson. (1981). Nimble fingers make cheap workers: An analysis of women's employment in third world export manufacturing. *Feminist Review, 7*, 87–107.

Fuller, C.J., & Narasimhan, H. (2007). Information technology professionals and the New-Rich middle class in Chennai (Madras), *Modern Asian Studies, 41*(1), 121–150.

Goetz, A. M., & Gupta, R. S. (1996). Who takes the credit? Gender, power and control over loan use in rural credit programs in Bangladesh. *World Development, 24*(1), 45–63.

Goodman, L. A. (1961). Snowball sampling. *Annals of Mathematical Statistics, 32*(1), 148–170.

Hakim, C. (1991). Grateful slaves and self made women: Fact and fantasy in women's work orientation. *European Sociological Review, 7*(2), 101–121.

Hakim, C. (1995). Five feminist myths about women's employment. *British Journal of Sociology, 46*(3), 429–455.

Hakim, C. (1996a). The sexual division of labor and women's heterogeneity. *British Journal of Sociology, 47*(1), 178–188.

Hakim, C. (1996b). *Key issues in women's work: Female heterogeneity and the polarization of women's employment*. London: Athlone.

Hirschbeerg, J. G., Maasoumi, E., & Slotje, D. J. (2001). Clusters of attribute and well-being in the USA. *Journal of Applied Econometrics, 16*, 445–460.

Hobijn, B., & Frances, P. H. (2000). Asymptotically perfect and relative convergences of productivity. *Journal of Econometrics, 15*, 59–81.

Inda, J.X., & Rosaldo, R. (2002). *The anthropology of globalization: A reader*. Basil Blackwell: Massachusets.

International Labour Organization. (2009). *Global employment trends for women, March 2009*. Geneva: International Labour Organization.

Kabeer, N. (1999). *The conditions and consequences of choice: Reflections on the measurement of women's empowerment*. UNRISD Discussion Paper 108. Geneva: United Nations Research Institute for Social Development.

Klassen, S. (2000). Measuring poverty and deprivation in South Africa. *Review of Income and Wealth, 46*, 33–58.

Kuklys, W. (2005). *Amartya Sen's capability approach: Theoretical insignts and empirical applications*. Berlin: Springer.

Lelli, S. (2001). *Factor analysis vs. fuzzy sets theory: Assessing the influence of different techniques on Sen's functioning approach*. KU Leuven: Center of Economic Studies, Discussion Paper, DPS 1.21.

Leavitt, H.J., & Whisler T.L. (1958). Management in the 1980s, *Harvard Business Review*, 11(Nov–Dec), 41–48.

Lim, L. Y. C. (1990). Women's work in export factories: The politics of a cause. In Irene Tinker (Ed.), *Persistent inequalities: Women and world development* (pp. 101–119). Oxford: Oxford University Press.

Maasoumi, E., & Nickelsburg, G. (1988). Multi-variate measures of well-being and an analysis of inequality in the Michigan data. *Journal of Business and Economic Statistics, 6*(3), 327–334.

Martinetti, E. C. (2000). A multidimensional assessment of well-being based on Sen's functioning approach. *Rivista Internazionale di Scienze Sociali, 2*, 207–239.

Mayoux, L. (1998). Participatory learning for women's empowerment in microfinance programmes: Negotiating complexity, conflict and change. *IDS Bulletin, 29*(4), 39–50.

Mcgee, V. E., & Carlton, W. T. (1970). Piecewise regression. *Journal of the American Statistical Association, 65*, 1109–1124.

Mitter, S., & Rowbotham, S. (Eds.). (1995). *Women encounter technology: Changing patterns of employment in the third world*. New York: Routledge.

Moser, C. O. N., & Clark, F. C. (Eds.). (2001). *Victims, perpetrators or actors? Gender, armed conflict and political violence*. London: Zed Books.

Narayan, D. (Ed.). (2005). *Measuring empowerment: Cross-disciplinary perspectives*. Washington, D.C.: World Bank.

NASSCOM. (2003). *The IT-BPO sector in India: Strategic review, 2003*. New Delhi: NASSCOM.

Nussbaum, M. C. (1988). Nature, function and capability: Aristotle on political distribution. *Oxford Studies in Ancient Philosophy, 6*, 145–184.

Nussbaum, M. C. (1990). Aristotelian social democracy. In B. Douglas, G. Mara, & H. Richardson (Eds.), *Liberalism and the God* (pp. 203–252). New York: Routledge

Nussbaum, M. C. (1995). Human capabilities, female human beings. In Martha C. Nussbaum & Jonathan Glover (Eds.), *Women, culture and development* (pp. 61–104). Oxford: Clarendon Press.

Nussbaum, M. C. (2000). *Women and human development: The capabilities approach*. Cambridge: Cambridge University Press.

Oxaal, Z., & Baden S. (1997). *Gender and empowerment: Definitions, approaches and implications for policy*. Brighton, UK: Briefing prepared for the Swedish International Development Cooperation Agency.

Oxfam, (1995). *The oxfam handbook of relief and development*. Oxford: Oxfam.

Parvin, G. A., Reazaul Ahsan, S. M., & Rahman Chowdhury, M. (2004). Women empowerment performance of income generating activities supported by rural women employment creation project (RWECP): A case study in Dumuria Thana, Bangladesh. *The Journal of Geo-Environment, 4*, 47–62.

Piccolo, D. (1970). A distance measure for classifying ARIMA Models. *Journal of Time Series, 11*, 153–164.

Qizilbash, M. (1998). The concept of well-being. *Economics and Philosophy, 14*, 51–73.

Qizilbash, M. (2002). A note on the measurement of poverty and vulnerability in the South African context. *Journal of International Development, 14*, 757–772.

Rahman, A. (1998). Micro-credit initiative for equitable and sustainable development: Who pays? *World Development, 26*(1), 67–82.

Raiser, M., Di Tomasso M. L., & Weeks M. (2000). *The measurement and determination of institutional change: Evidence from transition economics*. DAE Working Paper, 29.

Robeyns, I. (2003). Sen's capability approach and gender inequality: Selecting relevant capabilities. *Feminist Economics, 9*(2–3), 61–92.

Roemer, J. E. (1996). *Theories of distributive justice*. Cambridge: Harvard University Press.

Schokkaert, E., & Van Ootegem, L. (1990). Sen's concept of the living standard applied to the Belgian unemployed. *Recherches Economiques de Louvauin, 56*, 429–450.

Sen, A. K. (1983). Development: Which way now? *Economic Journal, 93*, 745–762.

Sen, A. K. (1984). *Resources, values and development*. Oxford: Basil Blackwell.

Sen, A. K. (1985). *Commodities and capabilities*. Oxford: Elsevier Science Publisher.

Sen, G., & Grown C. (1985). *DAWN, development, crises, and alternative visions: Third world womens perspectives*. New Delhi: Development Alternatives with Women for a New Era.

Sen, A. K. (1990a). Development as capability expansion. In K. Griffin & J. Knight (Eds.), *Human development and the international development strategy for the 1990s* (pp. 41–58). London: Macmillan.

Sen, A. K. (1990b). Gender and co-operative conflicts. In I. Tinker (Ed.), *Persistent inequalities: Women and world development* (pp. 129–149). New York: Oxford University Press.

Sen, A. K. (1992). *Inequality re-examined*. Oxford: Clarendon Press.

Sen, A. K. (1999). *Development as freedom*. New York: Anchor Books.

Sen, A. K. (2004). Capabilities, lists, and public reason: Continuing the conversation. *Feminist Economics, 10*(3), 77–80.

Shanker, D. (2008). Gender relations in IT companies. *Gender, Technology and Development, 12*(2), 185–202.

Simon, H.A. (1956). Rational choice and the structure of the environment. *Psychological Review, 63*(2), 129–138.

Srinivasan, T. N. (1994). Human development: A new paradigm or reinvention of the wheel? *American Economic Review, 84*(2), 238–243.

Sugden, R. (1993). Welfare, resources, and capabilities: A review of inequality reexamined by Amartya Sen. *Journal of Economic Literature, 31*, 1947–1962.

Swain, R. B. (2006). *Can microfinance empower women? Self-help groups in India. Mimeograph*. Uppsala: Department of Economics, Uppsala University.

UNDP. (1995). *Human development report 1995*. Oxford: Oxford University Press.

United Nations. (1995). *Report of the fourth world conference on women*, Beijing.

Williams, B. (1987). The standard of living: Interests and capabilities. In G. Hawthorn (Ed.), *The standard of living* (pp. 94–102). Cambridge: Cambridge University Press.

Williams, S., Seed, J., & Mwau, A. (1994). *Oxfam gender training manual*. Oxford: Oxfam.

World Bank. (2012). *Towards gender equality in East Asia and the Pacific*. Washington D.C.: The World Bank.

Ysander, B.-C. (1993). Robert Erikson: Descriptions of inequality. In Nussbaum, M. & Sen, A. K. (Eds.), *The quality of life*. Clarendon: Oxford University Press.

Zareen, F., & Khan, S. A. (2001). BRAC's microcredit programme: A case of Gohethra Sromojeebee women's co-operative. *Empowerment, Women for Women, 8*, 63–82.

Chapter 2
Women, Work and Exploitation: A Binary Perspective

Abstract In developing countries, policy makers commonly argue that involving women in paid economic activities is possibly the 'best' way of integrating women in development. This argument ignores the fact that the relations through which women are incorporated into the development process is crucial to understanding whether women's ability to shape and share values in the community is enhanced or inhibited. Pioneering empirical studies by Marxist researchers bring out this point, and are reviewed in this chapter to show how capitalism and patriarchy are interlinked and perpetually reinforce each other to subordinate women workers.

Keywords Capitalism · Patriarchy · Export-based industries

2.1 Introduction

A major concern among researchers on gender and policy makers in developing countries has been on how to involve women into the development process. The demand to 'integrate women in development' was initially raised in the International Women's Year Conference held in 1975 in Mexico City. Subsequently, it was echoed by international institutions and aid-giving agencies. It has been commonly accepted, based on Sen's capability approach, that involving women in (paid) economic activities is possibly the 'best' way of achieving this goal (Elson and Pearson 1981). Therefore, when structural adjustment programmes in development countries led to the entry of multinational corporations (MNCs) in export-based industries and created an increase in demand for workers, particularly women workers, it was expected that this would help in making women active partners in development.

Although the export-led industrialisation did involve women workers as key agents, development is a broad process, incorporating expansion of choices, access to resources that provide for life with dignity, and participation in decision-making (Fernandez Kelly 1981). In other words, it is not enough to incorporate women in

Z. Husain and M. Dutta, *Women in Kolkata's IT Sector*,
SpringerBriefs in Sociology, DOI: 10.1007/978-81-322-1593-6_2,
© The Author(s) 2014

development—we should also focus on the process of doing this. It implies that the relations through which women are incorporated in the development process is crucial to understanding whether the ability of women to shape and share values in the community process are enhanced or inhibited (Young 1984). This realisation has been the focus of considerable attention from Marxist scholars in the 1980s and 1990s. In this chapter we will review this literature.

2.2 Paid Work and Women's Agency

The Marxist literature on women's work and exploitation emerged as a criticism to the World Bank policies based on the assumption that employment will empower women. The hypothesised relation between paid work and women's agency may be understood in terms of Sen's work on development and freedom (Sen 1999). Sen starts by defining freedom as both the means and ends of development. The reason is that development has to be evaluated in terms of its impact on increasing or decreasing freedom, calling for a close analysis of the relationship between different types of freedoms and their levels. In particular, Sen argues, we should recognise that the level of freedom in one sphere (say social) may impinge upon the level of freedom in other spheres (for example, in the economic sphere). This will allow us to appreciate how social practices and the political-economic context affects one's ability to satisfy basic needs, perform various human functions and live flourishing lives.

A vital aspect of Sen's works is his focus on individuals as agents of change, rather than as recipients of development programmes. He argues that 'With adequate social opportunities, individuals can effectively shape their own destiny and help each other. They need not be seen as passive recipients of the benefits of cunning development programs' (Sen 1999, p. 11). Of particular importance is the issue of women's agency. It is vital not only for improving the socio-economic power of women, but for challenging and modifying entrenched values and social practices that support gender bias in the distribution of basic goods like food, shelter, education and health care. Moreover, women's agency has important externalities so that 'changing agency of women is one of the major mediators of economic and social change, and its determination as well as consequences closely relate to many of the central features of the development process' (Sen 1999, p. 202).

While the situating of the issue of measuring well-being within the sphere of women's control is undoubtedly welcome, controversy surrounds the policies that Sen recommends to enhance women's freedom and agency. He uses empirical studies to argue that women's agency is integrally connected to freedom in other domains such as freedom to work outside the home: 'freedom in one area (that of being able to work outside the household) seems to help foster freedom in others (enhancing freedom from hunger, illness, and relative to deprivation)' (Sen 1999, p. 194). Paid employment makes the women's contribution visible and recognisable, enhances her status and bargaining power within the household (so that she can demand her rights) and increases her social capital, thereby making her agency more effective.

This line of reasoning has been criticised by feminist researchers like Elson and Pearson (1981), Koggel (2003), Banerjee (1985, 1991, 1992) and others. They argue that such reasoning is simplistic—it overlooks the nature of market forces integrating women into the labour force and how the socio-cultural context moulds this process of integration. In the following section, we shall see the synergy between capitalism and patriarchy can involve women in economic activities without enhancing their agency. Of particular importance is the work on women workers in export-based industries.

2.3 Women, Patriarchy and Export-Led Industrialisation

Export-based manufacturing in the developing countries of Asia and Latin America began in the late 1950s. Domestic capital provided the initial impetus. Subsequently, foreign capital entered the field. The first country to start the export-based industrialisation drive was Hong Kong. The small size of the domestic economy as compared to its considerable industrial capacity (developed with the help of the capital and expertise of the refugees from Communist China) implied that industrialisation was constrained by the limited market. In a bid to break the shackles of the domestic demand constraint, Hong Kong embarked on a highly successful export drive, which set an example for other South-east Asian countries.

In the 1960s, Taiwan and South Korea, also, began to invest in locally owned import-substituting industries. The objective was to seek export outlets that would enable the expansion of productive capacity and ensure economies of scale. Meanwhile, across the Pacific, Mexico introduced the Border Industrialization Program (BIP). This programme was directed to establishing manufacturing units along the US border to generate employment and foreign exchange. The BIP successfully attracted many US firms, who relocated to Mexico.

The trend towards import-substituting industries was supported by governments in such countries. Policy makers in the early export manufacturing countries quickly realised that, given their import dependence and lack of protection in the form of quotas and tariff barriers, the export-based industries would not be able to survive in the highly competitive world market. To nurture these industries, inputs would have to be made available at world prices. The policy change led to the establishment of export processing or free trade zones where units were exempt from export and import duties, provided tax holidays and permitted 100 % foreign equity ownership.

Meanwhile, competition from such Asian countries and Japan forced capital in developed countries of Europe and North America to seek ways to cut costs and improve efficiency in high technology industries like semiconductor and other electronic components. One obvious strategy of doing so was to take advantage of the cheap labour supply in developing countries by relocating their plants to such countries—becoming MNCs.

Starting from the 1970s, therefore, capitalism witnessed what is called 'integrated transnational production' (Van Waas 1981). Sharp competition in the world markets led to MNCs in USA, Japan and West Germany to outsource the labour-intensive part of the production process to low wage areas, generally in developing countries like India, Bangladesh, Mexico, etc. Workers in such countries assemble parts supplied by parent corporations located in developed countries. After the labour-intensive processing is completed, they are exported for final processing and sale in the world market—referred to as New International Division of Labour (NIDL). Elson and Pearson (1981) argue that this is essentially a sophisticated version of the old 'putting-out' system, as the production process exported to developing areas are—apart from being labour-intensive—highly standardised and repetitious, and do not require much skill or knowledge.

Initially, only labour-intensive industries were relocated to developed countries. These industries—textiles, garments, footwear, toys and sporting goods—had simple production technologies. They were followed by firms manufacturing more sophisticated products like electrical household products and consumer electronics. In a third wave, hi-tech and capital-intensive industries like the semiconductor industry entered the fray. Forced by competition within the industry, firms manufacturing semi-conductors relocated the labour-intensive stages of their production process to developing countries.

While the search for cheap labour to maximise profit in the face of intensifying competition is undoubtedly a key factor underlying this process, it would be simplistic to assume such integrated transnational production as the outcome of a reactive strategy on the part of MNCs in the face of low-cost import competition. Rather, Van Waas (1981) argues, this trend has been the outcome of the convergence of several distinct techno-economic processes occurring in both the North and the South.

For instance, advances in the technology of transportation and communication have made 'production increasingly autonomous from marketing' (Young 1984, p. 387). Empirical evidence in support of this general tendency of disintegration, initially identified by Vernon (1966) in his product cycle theory, is provided by Van Waas (1981). Braverman (1974) also points out the importance of simplification of job tasks in stimulating integrating transnational production. In processes that are difficult or expensive to mechanise, or where the organisational process is changing so rapidly that it is costly to invest in technology, sub-division or 'de-skilling' of the labour process has occurred. In such situations relocation of manufacturing processes to low wage areas became an increasingly attractive option for MNCs,

Such relocation is also welcome to governments in such countries as it fits in with the strategy of export-led industrialisation that facilitates tackling of two policy objectives simultaneously, viz. generating employment and keeping balance of payments deficit within manageable limits. Consequently, governments in many developing countries attempted to promote the development and expansion of assembly operations (Van Waas 1981). Pressure from international aid agencies, like the World Bank and International Monetary Fund, to earn foreign exchange to repay their debts was another contributory factor in some countries. In this model, MNCs supply capital, technology, raw materials, managerial skill and a guaranteed market for the output, while the government ensures a friendly climate by investing in infrastructure, creating appropriate labour laws to ensure a tractable labour and offering tax incentives. The existence of free trade or export processing zones—originally set up to ensure the competitiveness of domestic export-based units to provide domestic units with cheap imported inputs—was another important factor.

2.3.1   Women and New International Division of Labour

The importance of ensuring a tractable labour force to ensure the sustainability of such transnational production processes has been addressed by several researchers (Elson and Pearson 1981; Lim 1978; Van Waas 1981). Van Waas (1981), in particular, has sought to explore the connection between the need to control labour and their choice of women to fill the majority of the assembly workforce. Lim (1978) points out that assembly operation require 'workers with low skills, a low level of commitment to the labour force, willingness to work for very low pay, and lack of union organisation' (Lim 1978, p. 4). These are perceived to be characteristics of women workers (Safa 1981). Furthermore, MNCs view women as 'bearers of inferior labour' (Young 1984, p. 389) they equate women's work with unskilled work (Elson and Pearson 1981). In other words, gender stereotyping of work leads to the large-scale employment of women workers in export-based industries.

2.3.2   'Nimble Fingers' and Cheap Labour

In contrary, Elson and Pearson (1981, p. 92) point out that it is not enough to simply note that jobs are stereotyped—researchers should also try to explain the reason for such stereotyping. For instance, researchers should explain why unemployment of male workers has failed to drive down wages and force them to accept employment in women's work.

Elson and Pearson argue:

> The reproduction in world market factories of the sexual division of labour typical in labour-intensive assembly operations in developed countries must therefore rest upon some differentiation of the labour force which makes it profitable to employ female labour

than male labour in these jobs. *Female labour must be either cheaper to employ than comparable male labour, or have higher productivity, or some combination of both; the net result being that unit costs of production are lower with female labour* (1981, p. 92).

Direct comparisons between male and female workers are hard to make, given the scarcity of male workers in similar jobs. Nevertheless, there is some evidence that women's wages in export-based units are 20–30 % lower than that of their male counterparts (Frobel et al. 1979). Studies of Malaysian electronics factories and Malawi textile factories also reveal that productivity of male workers is substantially lower than that of female workers. The question that naturally arises is: what produces this differentiation?

Sokoloff (1980) argues that it is necessary to understand the synergistic relationship between capitalism and patriarchy in order to answer this question. She argues that the labour market is organised to serve the interests of not only capitalists, but also of men. The consequent interrelationship between male power (embodied in a patriarchal society) and capitalism, therefore, has important implications for women's workforce participation pattern, their agency and resultant welfare. The systematic recruitment of women into low status, low-paid female-dominated occupations in industries with low capital, poor job mobility and limited job security is a blatant manifestation of this relationship. Sokoloff continues that attempts to understand women's position in the labour market must focus on her position within the home. Further, it is necessary to examine how patriarchal relations are 'transformed and intensified within the labour market' (1980, p. 13). This is required as patriarchy not confined to the household sphere (where we can observe private forms of individual male control over women), but operates within the labour market also. In the latter sphere, Sokoloff argues, patriarchy is manifested in '*collective* forms of male domination in the larger public society' (1980, p. 166). This implies that entry into the labour market may weaken *individual* forms of male control, but places women under *collective* forms of male domination. The latter is justified on the basis of perceived innate characteristics of female workers (Elson and Pearson 1981) and a calculated trivialisation of women's work and culture (Bell 1981).

Industrialists and policy makers commonly believe that the differentiation is natural (produced by innate capacities and personality traits of male and female workers) and by an objective differentiation of their income needs (in the sense that men work to support their families, while women merely supplement income earned by male members of the household). For instance, women workers are considered to have naturally nimble fingers, and are inclined to be more docile, willing to accept work discipline and less likely to unionise. This makes them naturally suited for tedious, repetitive and monotonous work.

Their lower wages—in spite of these natural advantages—are attributed to their role of mother within families. As Sokoloff (1980) argues, all women enter the labour market as 'mothers'—former, actual or potential. This is also true for the mainly young women who work in the factories. Their potential 'motherhood' implies that they will either be unwilling or unable to continue to work beyond their twenties. Although such 'natural wastage' actually benefits the export-based firms—as they can periodically vary the size of their labour force, keeping with fluctuations in demand for their output in the world market—this trend is used by a patriarchal society to label women workers as unreliable.

2.3.3 How Natural is this Differentiation?

Elson and Pearson (1981) argue that this differentiation is far from natural and inherited from their mothers. Rather the nimble hands and manual dexterity is the result of forces promoting gender segregation in work. From their infancy, girls are trained by their mothers and other female relatives in tasks that are socially appropriate to women's role. For instance, as the industrial sewing of clothes closely resemble sewing of clothes with a domestic sewing machine, girls trained in the latter 'naturally' possess the prized manual dexterity and capacity for spatial assessment required to perform such tasks efficiently. Similarly, training in needlework and sewing creates aptitude to perform other assembly-based industrial tasks:

> … manual dexterity of a high order may be required in typical sub-contracted operations, but nevertheless the operation is usually one that can be learned quickly on the basis of traditional skills. Thus, in Morocco, in six weeks, girls (who may not be literate) are taught the assembly under magnification of memory planes for computers—this is virtually darning with copper wire, and sewing is a traditional Moroccan skill. In the electrical field the equivalent of sewing is putting together wiring harnesses; and in metal working, one finds parallels in some forms of soldering and welding (Sharpston 1976, p. 334).

Although the work generally undertaken by women workers require a high degree of skill and competence, the fact that training can be imparted easily and within a short period for women workers to become proficient has an important implication. The skill of the women workers is derided as being naturally acquired, so that it becomes easier to classify them as being unskilled or semi-skilled labour. Patriarchy constructs skill categories in a subjective way so that jobs identified as typically women's work are classified as unskilled; on the other hand, work typically perceived to be men's work are considered to be skilled (Phillips and Taylor 1980). Thus, 'women do not do "unskilled" jobs because they are the bearers of inferior labour; rather the jobs they do are 'unskilled' because women enter them already determined as inferior bearers of labour' (Elson and Pearson 1981, p. 94).

Given that they are supposedly bearers of inferior labour, women are often ascribed 'secondary status' in the labour market (Lim 1978, p. 11). Wages paid to them are lower than that of male workers, so that 'the wages earned (by female workers) are often insufficient to support a family' (Lim 1978). Thus, although women work as the single income (earned by their father) may fail to support the family, their contribution to family income in monetary terms is less than that of male workers. This allows the idea that it is male members who supports the family to remain unchallenged.

2.3.4 *Mirage of Emancipation*

The hybrid of patriarchy and capitalism, therefore, renders women a reserve labour force—if they are active in the labour market, they serve to increase consumption levels in the economy, but they do not compete against men for high paid jobs. Nor does participation in economic activities benefit women at home. Their secondary status in the labour market implies that women workers are unable to acquire the attributes of 'free wage labour', viz. the worker has the freedom to sell his labour power as his own commodity and is free of all the objects needed for the reali-sation of his labour power (Marx 1976). Elson and Pearson maintain that a woman is never 'free' in this sense:

> She has the obligations of domestic labour, difficulties in establishing control over her own body, an inability to be fully a member of society in her own right; but also the possibility of obtaining her subsistence from men in exchange for personal services of a sexual or nurturing kind, of realising her labour power outside the capitalist labour process (1981, p. 97).

Such issues are conveniently swept aside or ignored by liberals who argue that the entry of women into factories ensures their financial independence and will empower them over time. They further argue that—given the faceless nature of market transactions—discrimination in the labour market will be a transient phenomenon. Traits like manual dexterity, docility and readiness to be trained may render women workers cheaper to employ initially. In the long run, the consequent high rates of male unemployment will undermine such 'natural' distinctions as male workers are forced to assume the attributes that makes women attractive as workers. In the long run, therefore, the labour force becomes undifferentiated by gender—both men and women perform same jobs and under identical working conditions.

The fact that the traits are socially acquired and the product of gender dis-crimination under patriarchy in the social sphere—and so cannot be acquired by men—are overlooked. Nor are the multiple ways through organisation of work and incentive structure reinforce patriarchal gender subordination considered.[1] Even when personal kinship-based gender subordination is destroyed, this does not benefit women workers who become subordinate to male bosses. The absence of kinship elements in such relations permits the introduction of sexuality in the worker–employer relationship, lowering the respectability of factory girls. Sexual exploitation is not uncommon. For instance, there have been reports of such harassment by Japanese supervisors in Masan Free Export Zone in South Korea. Given its frailty and susceptibility to external shocks, often emanating from distant economies, this new form of gender subordination is highly unstable. Conditions

---

[1] For instance, some of the American electronics MNCs provide lessons in fashion and beauty, and organise fashion shows, Western dances and social functions for their employees. Such fringe benefits are interpreted as encouraging commoditized forms of marriage by Elson and Pearson (1981).

like pregnancy or occupational ailments are used as excuses to retrench workers and adjust its size to demand conditions. In such cases, the retrenched workers are bereft of the protection provided by the traditional form of gender subordination to male relatives. In South Korea, Grossman (1979) reports, many former electronics worker has been forced into prostitution after retrenchment.

2.4 Women in Export-Based Industries: Selected Case Studies

In this section, we will briefly review four case studies to see how patriarchy and capitalism interacts with the local context to create mirages of inclusive development for women.

2.4.1 Maquiladoras in Mexico[2]

Maquiladoras are textile, electronics and machinery-assembly factories located in low wage regions in which workers assemble imported materials for export. The maquiladoras developed as part of the 1965 BIP of the Mexican government. This policy was adopted in response to the Mexican government's interest in taking advantage of the border economy to reduce unemployment and the US manufacturer's interest in locating cheap source of labour to assemble textile, electronics and machinery.

The history of the maquiladoras can be divided into three phases. During the first phase (1965–1974), the maquiladoras grew rapidly, based on a largely female workforce. The capitalist exploitation of women in this phase was based on the subordination of women within the family by the patriarchal nature of Mexican society. Although the economic needs of their families forces women to work (Fernandez Kelley 1983)—in fact, the periodic unemployment of male members often makes the contribution of these women workers crucial for the survival of the family—this is not acknowledged by the maquiladora management, or even within their own family. The latter contend that women workers do *not* support their families—they merely supplement income earned by male members. The deliberate devaluation of women's work justifies the positioning of women in dead end jobs with low pay as they have limited career aspirations and financial responsibilities. The traditional marginality of women also helps the management to undertake periodic lay-offs. In such cases, women workers voluntarily resign at the end of their (3 or 6 months) contracts and are replaced by fresh workers. Only if demand conditions are favourable, are they rehired next day at starting wages.

---

[2] Based on Fussell (2000) and Young (1984).

There is no provision for any severance pay. This implies that women basically form a highly flexible reserve labour whose size can be adjusted, smoothly and without cost, in tune with fluctuations in world market demand.

Recession and growing militancy of Mexican labour (Sklair 1993) ended the period of rapid growth in 1974. To tackle the latter problem, the Mexican government introduced a series of labour market reforms to discipline labour and control wage growth. This reassured US manufacturers, so that moderate growth occurred in the late 1970s. The Mexican crisis of 1982, coupled with devaluation of the Mexican currency, led to the onset of the third phase in maquiladora growth. The economic crisis increased the commitment of the government to trade liberalisation as a means of economic recovery, while devaluation of the peso lowered wages in real terms.

Over this period, important changes occurred in the gender composition of the labour force and their social characteristics. In the first phase, nearly 80 % of maquiladora workers were women. Moreover, these women were young, single, childless and relatively more educated migrant women (Fernandez Kelley 1983; Brannon and Lucker 1990), chosen mainly for their docility and manual dexterity (Sklair 1993; Tiano 1994). From the 1980s, increased demand for labour created demand in excess of the supply of labour from young, single and childless women. This led to increasing masculinisation of the workforce, with the proportion of female workers dropping from 77 % (1982) to 41 % (1999)—even though there was an increase in female workers in absolute terms (from 0.10 to 0.75 million between 1982 and 1999). This process was encouraged by technological progress within the maquiladoras, creating demand for more skilled, masculine labour force. Even within the female workforce, there was a major change in the social characteristics, with a shift from working daughters to working mothers. One reason was that women with families had more to loose from militancy. Such women, therefore, were now considered to be ideal prototype of cheap labour (Tiano 1994; Standing 1999).

Using Labour Trajectories Survey (LTS) Fussell (2000) employs multivariate methods to test whether maquiladora wages is higher than that in other domestic sectors. She finds that, even after controlling for education and duration in current job, significant differences exist in wages across occupational categories, with maquiladora wages being lower than that in commerce and service sector employment and earnings of self-employed workers.

Analysis of the impact of individual traits like education, age, marital status and number of children on duration of current job gives results consistent with what feminist literature leads us to expect. Single women, those who are childless, or do not have very small children are more likely to be able to hold on to their work. There is no evidence to suggest that maquiladora workers' competing family responsibilities diminish their commitment to work. Only for the 12–19 years aged workers does age affect job duration. Being married or having a child is not an important factor in determining security of tenure. This is consistent with feminist research (Tiano 1994; Barajas and Sotomayor 1995) arguing that women workers in maquiladoras are dependent on their wages, compared to workers in other sectors.

Another important issue is the choice of sectors in which the women seek employment. Apart from market conditions, the demographic and household characteristics of women workers are important in determining in which sector—in maquiladoras, service or commerce sectors or as self-employed workers—they end up. Women with greatest advantages in labour market should end up in the lucrative jobs, while those who are least attractive to employers end up in low paying sectors, or have to be self-employed. The classification of women workers by occupations, household traits and demographic characteristics, therefore, provides an indication of which traits are attractive to prospective employers.

Such analysis reveals that the profile of maquiladora workers have changed over time. They are now slightly older, poorly educated women with young children. This finding supports Tiano's (1994) hypothesis that, since the recession, maquiladora employers are trying to target a more disadvantaged section of the workforce who are in greater need of the income from working in the maquiladora plants. MNCs are targeting older women with families characterised by many dependents but few workers. Such women are experiencing the greatest economic squeeze, and cannot afford the luxury of waiting in the hope for higher paid jobs in the service and commercial sector in the future. As a result, these women are forced to accept the poor wages and working conditions offered to them.

2.4.2 Strawberry Farming in Mexico[3]

The strawberry agri-business in Zamora, Mexico, began to expand in the mid-1960s. Initially, it was based on US capital; subsequent, domestic capital funded growth of the industry. Two factors contributed to the competitiveness of the Mexican strawberry firms in the international market—the fact that they grow in the winter and their low costs (particularly, transport and labour costs). There were 18 plants in Zamora and the adjacent village of Jacona in 1979–1980, the period of study. There were minor fluctuations in hiring characteristics and in work and pay conditions across the firms.

Women were recruited by the firms at an early age. Generally, they joined the workforce when they were 12–15 years of age. As a result, the majority of workers are inexperienced.[4] They generally continue working till their marriage; this takes place when they are 17–20 years. Those who do not marry continue working. Among married women, very few return to work. These workers are generally divorced, or separated from husbands, or widowed. Most of the unmarried girls live with their parents or family members. This is partly because of social norms restricting girls residing alone. The housing shortage in the area is also responsible.

---

[3] Based on Arizpe and Aranda (1981).

[4] Among those respondents who had previous work experience, 56 per cent had worked in agriculture and 31 per cent before joining the strawberry firms.

Wages are handed over to parents, who return some money periodically to enable the workers to meet their personal expenses. The money retained is used to buy household consumer goods, which imparts social status and prestige. It also serves as an asset that may be sold or used as security to secure a loan during financial crisis. The survey found that 62 % of the respondents provided partial support to their family. Only one out of five were the major income earning members in their families.

Arizpe and Aranda (1981) investigated the reasons why strawberry plants preferred hiring girls. Managers stated that women workers had higher productivity; they were also ''very quick with their hands'' and ''concentrate better than men' (Arizpe and Aranda 1981, p. 462). While it is true that removing stems and selecting strawberries requires a manual dexterity that few men possess, this is not the real reason why firms prefer women workers. The main reason, Arizpe and Arande argue, is that the socio-cultural context of the region—like rapid population growth, family structure and culture assigning women a subordinate position within the family—creates comparative disadvantages of young women. Agribusiness capital takes advantage of such disadvantages to reduce cost, thereby increasing their own international competitiveness in the world market. Two factors help MNCs to reduce wage costs by exploiting women workers.

First, agro-industry cannot compete with wages paid in US. This leads to outmigration of male workers. Women workers, on the other hand, do not have other more attractive alternative. Within the locality, they generally find work either as agricultural labourer or as domestic helps. In both cases, they are paid lower wages. It is true that urban wages are higher; here cultural restrictions on the migration of women come into play. This results in a situation where women workers have no alternative but to accept the low wages and poor working conditions in the strawberry industry.

The second way in which hiring of women workers helps to minimise the wage bill is through the high rates of turnover among women workers. Frequent dropping out from work observed among women workers due to marriage or childbirth or due to other family-related reasons results in considerable savings in wages as firms do not have to pay increments, maternity benefits, disability benefits or pension. Moreover, it facilitates trimming of the labour force to ensure compatibility with demand in the world market. Another advantage of high labour turnovers is that it prevents the accumulation of information, experience and social capital that might have been used to organise trade unions and demand better pay and working conditions.

Not surprisingly, therefore, entry into the labour market has failed to produce radical social changes or substantially improve the lot of women in the region. Residential patterns have remained unchanged—with the majority of women workers continuing to reside with their families. Some do stay apart from their parents—with other relatives—but remain subject to same restrictions and conditions of domination as in their parents' household. There has been a marginal increase in personal consumption. Most of the women workers still hand over their wages to parents, or spend on family needs. Although women workers have more freedom of movement, this freedom is subject to certain restrictions. The threat of harassment by men in the streets reduces the de facto mobility of women workers. Hence, their movements to and fro from their residence to place of work have to be monitored by recruiters and union leaders.

The only positive development has been in terms of higher aspirations. Women exercise greater choice in choice of husbands. Some of they also express a desire to get educated and move ahead in life. But, the absence of incentives for human capital augmentation in the strawberry plants, the instability of employment and poor pay means that these aspirations remain pipe dreams. Instead of producing social change, the economic context results in a condition where workers are simply pushed back into the traditional role of wife-mother instead of trying for material movement. In fact, there is the danger that, if the strawberry industry collapses, the mismatch between aspirations and the means to attain them will produce misfits of the relatively emancipated women.

2.4.3 Women Workers in India's Informal Sector

The Indian experience, too, has been remarkably similar to that observed in East Asian countries and Mexico. 'Family …and the rituals that have gone into marriage, and the rules of behaviour, and the role allocation that have been spelt out, sometimes provide an impossible barrier to equality between the sexes' (Jain and Banerjee 1985, p. 9). Further, '… in our society, the inadequate recognition and low evaluation of women's role in the households has been the major factor contributing to the generally low status and welfare of women' (Jain and Banerjee 1985, p. 16). Jain and Banerjee observe that growing poverty and stagflation forced into the labour force a large number of women who had neither any training for the job market, nor any preparedness for such work. Being less trained, less informed and more desperate than men, they were willing to accept the dregs of the labour market.

Such women face two kinds of discrimination in the labour market: (a) women are paid less for identical tasks and (b) women are confined to a limited number of relatively inferior tasks. The identification of tasks as typically meant to be performed by women resulted in a degradation of its value. Thus, social rating of any task was determined by which sex performed it, and not the value of the end product.

It was further observed that activities performed by women used and using crude tools, mostly based on manual energy. As a result production tends to be slow, and the product non-standardised. Thus, women's skill was actually a substitution of women's energy for capital and energy. Historically, women were eliminated whenever mechanisation was introduced in factories. This was among the chief cause of the secular decline in the manufacturing employment of the Indian women between 1911 and 1961. Even in export-based industries, where employment of women accelerated in the 1980s, the increase was mainly due to the use of labour-intensive technology in certain processes.

In the informal sector, where a large part of the female workforce is located, fierce competition did open the doors of traditionally male-dominated occupations (Banerjee 1985). But it also lowered wages; this was a major problem for women as they were shunted to less-skill intensive jobs, where pay is lower. It also enabled employers to force women workers to work in unhygienic and unsanitary conditions and deprived them of security of tenure, social security benefits and regular leave (Banerjee 1991).

Nor did employment empower women. Their low earnings implied that their contribution to family income, although crucial, remained peripheral (Banerjee 1992). As a result participation of women in the informal labour market failed to pull their household out of the poverty trap, so that their contributions remain under-valued. This prevented any positive spin-offs to women in the form of greater control over financial resources, or even of their income. Rather, their leisure time was severely affected as the women workers remained the suppliers of care services, aided at most by their minor children.

2.5 Exploitation of Women in Affluent Households

An important characteristic of the Marxist approach is that they have equated economic exploitation with exploitation in other spheres. Gender and class have, in their writings, become linked. This has led to an almost exclusive focus on exploitation of (economically) marginalised women from low income households. But women from affluent households too are subjugated by a patriarchal society and deprived of agency, even though these women may enjoy high consumption levels and earn large salaries. How these women are exploited is worth analysing.

2.5.1 The Issue of Care Services

In an etymological sense, care means to provide needed assistance or watchful supervision. Feminist researchers, on the other hand, use the term in a more specific way to refer to a sense of responsibility. Badgett and Folbre (2001) argue that a distinction between 'care services' (a type of work) and 'caring motives' (feelings intrinsic to a worker) is important. Care services are services involving a personal contact between provider and recipient. The provisioning of such services may be motivated by pecuniary or other instrumental interests. But, in many cases, a personal link with the recipient may develop, based on affection, altruism or social norms of obligation and respect. While assessing quality of care services it is necessary to consider such personal and emotional content.

2.5.2 Gender and the Assignment of Care Services

Care services within a family may be provided by either a formal care giver, or by family members. Since the former may be quite costly (England and Folbre 1999), in many cultures, of both developing and developed countries, women are typically assigned the burden of providing care services[5] for other family members. Gender segregation of care and wage-earning labour is achieved in two ways.

First, it is argued that the opportunity cost of providing care services is higher for males—as men are (the argument runs) more productive than females they are more likely to get work and earn higher wages than women workers. The second process is social. Providing care services requires agents (in this case, women) to deviate from self-interested behaviour. Such behaviour may involve incurring personal loss in order to benefit the recipient of care services. Such self-sacrifice may be coerced through social moulding of individual preferences.[6] Under patriarchy, socio-cultural norms and role models typically associate women with care services by portraying them as mother and wife and inculcating this sense through various learning and indoctrination processes like education, social interaction, games, etc. from childhood. 'Gender norms governing interpretation of appropriate behaviour for women and men are closely linked to socially constructed concepts of family altruism and individual self-interest' (Badgett and Folbre 2001, p. 327). The impact of such gendered structures of constraints (Folbre 1994) may be understood using a game theoretic framework.

Game theory is an approach commonly used by economists, political scientists, sociologists and researchers in other behavioural sciences to study interaction of agents (called players) in a situation of 'strategic interdependence'. Normally, the outcome or pay-off to an agent will depend upon her choice of strategy or actions. Strategic interdependence refers to a situation of mutual dependence—means that the choices and actions of each player will determine the outcome from the choice by the other player. Such games can be cooperative (players can negotiate to take a collective action when playing the game) or non-cooperative (players take decisions on their own, though they may recognise their strategic interdependence). The latter classes of games may assume different forms, depending upon the type of solution that is believed to be optimal. For instance, in games of coordination, it is best if players choose the same strategy. In games of anti-coordination—of which Game of Chicken is an important example—it is best if players choose different strategies.

---

[5] Care providers experience a significant reduction in lifetime earnings (Joshi 1990, 1998; Waldfogel 1997). Moreover, the skill acquired by a family member providing care services is generally not transportable to other markets. This adversely affects their bargaining ability within the family (Braunstein and Folbre 1999).

[6] Literature tends to focus on the role of norms as a solution to coordination problems. However, a norm may also "be conceived of as a sophisticated tool of coercion, used by the favoured party in a status quo of inequality to promote its interest in the maintenance of this status quo" (Ullmann-Margalit 1977, p. 189).

Fig. 2.1 Household chores
as a game of chicken

Husband / Wife	Do household tasks	Take rest
Do household tasks	(2, 2)	(1, 3)
Take rest	(3, 1)	(0, 0)

The Game of Chicken is a game derived from teenage virility rites. Two drivers race their cars across a bridge along the same lane, starting from opposite ends of the bridge. If any one driver (or both) deviates from the lane, then she is a chicken and looses her self-esteem. The winner is the driver who keeps to the lane. The risk is that if both drivers stick to their lanes, then they will crash. In this situation, if one driver can somehow signal (indicate) to the other driver that she will never deviate—damaging the steering wheel, for instance, or tying up her hands—then that driver can assure herself of winning as the best strategy for the other driver will then be to deviate and save her life.

Folbre and Weiskopf (1998) show that the issue of care services may be modelled in terms of the Game of Chicken.

In Fig. 2.1 we have pay-offs from providing care services to a working couple. A husband and wife return home from work, and find that they have to cook and wash the dishes. The individual options before the dyad is given by the two rows (for the wife) and by the two columns (for the husband). The return, or pay-off, obtained by adopting a particular option or strategy is given in the cells, with the first figure denoting pay-off to the wife and the second figure the pay-off to the husband. It is clear that the situation is characterised by strategic interdependence. Strategic interdependence means that pay-off to any player depends not only on what he(she) chooses, but on what the other person does. The pay-off resulting from the choice made by the couple is indicated by the cell corresponding to the relevant row and column chosen by the wife and husband, respectively. For instance, in our example, the couple can share the tasks, or one spouse can do the work alone. In the latter case, the person who has to do the work becomes even more tired, while the other person relaxes and gets a higher pay-off. There is another possibility—neither does the tasks, so that they both go to bed hungry.

Now the solution to this game is referred to as *Nash equilibrium*. This is defined as follows: given the choice of the other person, each agent chooses the strategy that maximises her pay-off.[7] Note that this must simultaneously hold for both players. For instance, if the husband throws himself down on a sofa and announces that he is too tired to do the household chores, the wife can either follow suit (and get a pay-off of 0) or do the chores herself (in which case her pay-off is 1). Obviously, it is better for her to do the chores herself. In that case, neither player

---

[7] In other words, "an outcome ... is said to be a Nash equilibrium if no player would find it beneficial to deviate provided that all other players do not deviate from their strategies played at the Nash outcome" (Shy 1995, p. 18).

Wife \ Husband	Do household tasks	Take rest
Do household tasks	$(2 + \theta, 2)$	$(1+ \theta, 3)$
Take rest	$(3-\theta, 1)$	$(-\theta, 0)$

Fig. 2.2 Household chores as a game of chicken under patriarchy

has the incentive to deviate from the equilibrium given in the north-east cell. This is a Nash equilibrium.

The problem, given the symmetrical nature of the matrix, is that there is another Nash equilibrium at the south-west cell. If the wife commits herself to taking rest, the best option before the husband is to do the work himself. The question then arises: which Nash equilibrium will prevail. In the presence of multiple Nash equilibria, no solution will emerge. In fact, it is quite possible that both players may decide to take rest and go to bed hungry.

Now avoiding household tasks is not sustainable in the long run as both persons will starve. To ensure a Nash solution that is also practically feasible we must introduce social norms. Under patriarchy, for instance, it is the social responsibility of the wife to perform household chores. Given that the wife internalises this norm, the pay-off matrix will be modified (Fig. 2.2), making the game matrix asymmetric. Assume that, under patriarchy, the wife gains an additional pay-off of (say) θ for adherence to social norms by doing the household chores herself, and is penalised by θ for not doing the work herself. It can be seen that if θ is positive, in this case, the equilibrium in the north-east cell represents a Nash equilibrium. The south-west cell (wife taking rest, while husband does the chores) is no longer Nash equilibrium as—given the husband's decision to work—the wife can improve her pay-off by sharing in the chores. This outcome is also not a new Nash equilibrium. The reason is that the husband will stop working and take rest—so that the family ends up in the north-east cell. The presence of patriarchal relations, therefore, modifies the pay-offs in the Game of Chicken from Figs. 2.1 to 2.2 and results in a stable Nash equilibrium—with the wife doing the household chores and the husband taking rest.

Now, social norms are not static and have to be created; they also evolve over time. Let us now see how such norms were created and how socio-economic changes affect their stability.

2.5.3 Changing Forms of the Family

Young and Wilmott (1973) argue that the family in Western society has evolved over the years, starting from family as a production unit. In this phase, all family members worked within the home, being engaged in agricultural land attached to the home, in home-based factories, rearing children and other activities. In this phase, the home was the centre of all activities, economic or otherwise.

In the second phase, the home-centred family broke down. Income earning activities occurred outside the home. Although women were not debarred from participating in such activities, the gendered segregation of family labour constrained them to remain within the home to take care of children and undertake other household chores. The norm assigning women with the sole responsibility of providing care services emerged at this time. Further, the gender segregation, along with the fact that children are potential future workers, meant that there was no incentive to control fertility. This created a situation that may be conceptualised in terms of Fig. 2.2.

Starting from the end of the nineteenth century women began to understand their body and acquire knowledge about the physical processes, particularly those relating to fertility. Women started to control fertility by refusing to have intercourse during periods of fertility. Along with the emergence of new forms of contraception, legislation restricting child labour and the introduction of compulsory schooling increased the costs of having children and reduced fertility trends. This also reduced the opportunity costs of women working, so that they started returning to the labour market after children became old enough to take care of themselves. Female workforce participation rates started increasing, increasing contribution of women to household income.

Simultaneously, there were other forces that cemented the family in its new role as a consumption unit. Fewer children and higher wages made the home environment pleasant. The introduction of household aids and appliances such as electric refrigerators, stoves, washing machines, vacuum cleaners and other home tools changed the nature of housework by not only making them less tedious and labour-intensive than before, but also more interesting to men. This broke down traditional barriers segregating men and women in different spheres and type of work. In terms of the earlier games, the disutility from doing the household chores decreases, modifying the pay-offs. The incentive to 'defect' by not doing the household chores and resting reduces, so that an equilibrium with both partners sharing household chores becomes more likely.

Moreover, as pointed out by Carnoy (2001), the increasing returns to (higher) education, in the form of access to high paying jobs, further affected the nature of the family. Investing in children would allow them to earn more than their parents and move up the consumption ladder. This implied that, in addition to a consumption unit, the family became an investment unit. Demand side conditions in the labour market—requiring a steady flow of educated and skilled force—was also important in this context.

The evolution of the family as a consumption and investment unit increased the importance of women as an income earner. The impact on the role of women as provider of care services was less specific. While the double burden on women continued, the increased recognition of their economic and other contribution to the family led women to challenge the patriarchal norms consigning the undertaking of all household duties to women. This would imply a return to the structure shown in Fig. 2.1. In this framework, we have seen, two possible equilibria are possible—with either both partners working, or with none working.

The specific outcome was context dependent. In societies where men were prepared to participate in household chores, facilitated by the introduction of mechanical aids, the contraction of women's labour in the household sphere occurred smoothly. In other cases, the search for substitutes in the form of hired providers of household services became an important issue. The costs of such providers, their acceptability within the family and the pattern of integration into the household determined the extent to which such substitution could occur. In some cases, women were unable to discard the responsibilities of undertaking household chores and were forced to undertake the double shift. In others, the successful shifting of the responsibility for providing care services to hired substitutes led to women shifting to a supervisory role within the household domain. In game theoretic terms, the pay-offs to not working increased—as someone else was doing the household chores, while both partners were resting. This reduced role conflict, while providing welcome relief to such women.

Women's involvement in the labour market had another important effect:

> Women wanted broader options, including participation in the social world defined by work and greater decision-making power over the larger issues in family life, including the division of family labour. Women's rising access to remunerative work increased their chances of gaining some economic independence from men (Carnoy 2001, p. 312).

Two separate working schedules, along with awareness among women backed by greater bargaining power within the household, increased friction within the family and affected the stability of marriage as an institution. In Western societies, this led to a rapid rise in the divorce rates and emergence of new forms of consumption partnerships that are less institutionalized and stable than marriage. Such trends have also spilled over to Asian countries. Studies report that divorce rates in South-east and East Asian countries have increased since the 1980s (Jones 2007; Lee 2006). In India, lawyers report, they get substantially more divorce and separation cases than before—particularly from affluent households. Analysis of the Socio-Cultural Tables in the 2001 Census reveals that 7.1 % of urban women are divorced or separated; this figure has increased to 8.4 % in 2009 (Sample Registration Survey 2009 figures). Ironically, the increasing instability of marriage in upper middle class Indian society is leading to increased entry of women into the labour market, with employment being seen as a form of insurance against the possible dissolution of marriage.

2.5.4 The Mommy Track

While developments in the home front provided some relief to women, in the workplace patriarchy still reigned. Increasing entry of women into the labour market meant that men now had to face greater competition for entry and for promotion. Both challenged the traditional superiority of men and, in turn, weakened their control over the family. Since movements by women demanding equal rights in the labour market reduced the scope for discrimination at the entry level, patriarchy had to respond in a subtle way. The response was in the form of emphasising femininity and its associated care providing functions, which debarred women workers from a full time commitment to work.

One way of doing this is through the propagation of 'male' patterns of work (Coyle 1989). Firms demand a fast track career pattern consisting of recruitment of graduates and rapid acquisition of skills and experience in order to consolidate their careers by the early thirties. Such career patterns calls for long hours and do not take into account child bearing and childcare responsibilities. Management argue that women will be unable to participate fully in work activities because of their domestic responsibilities, leading to what Greenhaus and Beutell (1985) call family-to-work conflict. A traditional myth in management has been that such conflict is greater for women (Pleck 1977; Dilworth 2004; Crouter 1984), with such conflict intensifying for women with children below 6 years or with elderly care responsibilities. Managerial competence, therefore, becomes inevitably linked to masculinity.

Those women who compromised on their work schedule to fulfil their household responsibilities were shirkers—they are treated with ridicule for conforming to the patriarchal perception of inefficient women. Sümer et al. (2008) cite the case of Bridget, a 24-year old mother of two children, who used to work at a call centre. After returning to work, Bridget found her manager and colleagues unsympathetic to her need for flexibility. For instance, when she took leave during her daughter's illness, her manager was critical. Bridget had to miss her daughter's 6 month health review because '... they would not let me have the day's leave and they just weren't very flexible...'. On the other hand, traditional division of household work and ideology about the respective roles of partners created a sense of guilt within women workers: 'And you know ... always feeling guilty about work, always feeling guilty about your child, all that kind of stuff' (interview with Barbara, cited by Sümer et al. (2008, p. 376)).

Nor is the lot of women workers who did not conform to the traditional (patriarchal) image but were prepared to work at par with their male colleagues substantially better. Such women are defeminised and accused of neglecting their family and children. They were considered to be sexless and unattractive, while their careerism was interpreted as a modern manifestation of their inherent irresponsibility. Their high visibility in the workplace only created isolation. Cooper and Davidson (1982) report that women managers have to face constant questioning about their commitment and competence from their colleagues. The majority of women managers face indifferent and patronising behaviour; in some cases, male colleagues are hostile to and may even harass the women managers. A possible reason why male workers perceive women managers as greater threats to their own career growth and try to block their career growth is the departure of women from their culturally defined role of domestic care provider.

Caught between Scylla and Charbdis, women workers tend to avoid being isolated and sought security in numbers. This meant that the majority of women workers preferred to conform to the traditional role of care provider—although, in many cases, this role was modified to supervisor of care services—and focussed more on family responsibilities than on work. Compromises were sought in the latter domain through early hours, reluctance to undertake over time or undertake assignments involving overnight stay and other such means. These compromises, in turn, affect their career prospects—either slowing vertical movement significantly, or leading to cul-de-sacs. This outcome is sometimes called the 'mommy track' (Schwarz 1989).

The mommy track refers to the shunting off of women with family responsibilities into dead end low paying jobs. Schwartz's (1989) article in the *Harvard Business Review* first drew attention to the 'mommy track' phenomenon. Schwartz claimed that while 'the cost of employing women in management is greater than the cost of employing men', this greater cost is due primarily to gendered expectations of the workplace and women's duties in raising children. Schwartz wrote:

> The misleading metaphor of the glass ceiling suggests an invisible barrier constructed by corporate leaders to impede the upward mobility of women beyond the middle levels. A more appropriate metaphor, I believe, is the kind of cross-sectional diagram used in geology. The barriers to women's leadership occur when potentially counterproductive layers of influence on women—maternity, tradition, socialisation—meet management strata pervaded by the largely unconscious preconceptions, stereotypes, and expectations of men. Such interfaces do not exist for men and tend to be impermeable for women (Schwartz 1989).

2.6 Women Workers in India's IT Sector

In India, the abandonment of *license raj* and shift to a more liberalised economy linked to global markets had begun in the 1980s, and gained pace in the subsequent decade. The relaxation of Foreign Direct Investment (FDI) in India allowed the entry of MNCs into the economy. Policy changes, along with the expansion of markets for Indian goods and services abroad, led to the diffusion of a global corporate culture at the high end of the Indian manufacturing and service sector. Such 'cultural globalisation', particularly the introduction of the IT sector, was expected to create a space where the employment would lead to empowerment.

2.6.1 Birth of a Hope

Initial hopes about the empowering effect of the IT sector were based on the nature of technological change in the IT sector. Such changes led to the development of what Gaio (1995) calls the 'soft' side of technology. Innovations like replacement of the mainframes by smaller processor platforms using the QWERTY keyboards and increasing role of communication-related components have led to closer interaction between consumers and producers. Women enjoy a comparative advantage in such one-to-one (often faceless) communication channels as they have a more attractive voice-based communication style and are generally more patient and diligent.

Simultaneously, innovations in communication technology have made fragmentation of the work process technically possible. Such fragmentation allows part of the work process (generally involving no decisions, or low-level decision-making) to be undertaken in offshore locations where labour costs are substantially lower. The spread of IT in fields like insurance, banking, telecommunications, health and tourism has created demand for a computer literate workforce often outstripping the supply of such workers. Companies can no longer afford the luxury of gender discrimination. In fact, women workers are not only treated on equal terms, but accorded preference due to the notion that 'women are more docile and less likely to unionise or demand better wages' (Poonacha and Rajan 1996).

As a result women are gradually becoming 'core agents in the technical and social changes necessary for the further diffusion of information technologies' (Gaio 1995 p. 226). In Brazil, for instance, Gaio (1995) notes that women workers account for almost half of the IT sector workforce, and have fared better than in traditional professional jobs.

There are also Indian studies confirming the positive effect of employment in IT sector on empowerment and agency. Clarke and Sekher (2007) argue that growth of the IT sector has led to a partial reversal of the tendency to devalue a daughter within Indian families. Shanker (2008) notes a tendency for social relations to become more gender neutral within and outside the workplace.

In recent times, some researchers (viz. Mitter and Rowbotham 1995; COD 2004; Upadhyay 2005) have become more critical of the effect of the IT sector on empowerment of women. Such studies focus on how the corporate culture characterising the IT sector has evolved in Indian society, which still remains a bastion of patriarchy. It is argued that the cocktail of capitalism and patriarchy has resulted in new forms of gender discrimination, creating additional stress on women workers.

2.6.2 Working Women Within the Family

To understand the basis of their arguments it is necessary to approach the problem from a historical perspective. We start by looking at the reasons for entry of women workers into the labour market. The deterioration in standard of living after the Second World War, caused by hyper-inflation, had led to women from middle and low income families being allowed to join the labour force by the men within the family. Since the objective was to simply use women to augment family income, women were not freed from household responsibilities, or from adhering to the social norm of providing care services. They worked in fixed hours jobs, sacrificing their leisure hours to undertake domestic responsibilities. Social norms led to a gendered division of labour and designated women as the sole providers of care services, leading to a Nash equilibrium as described in Chap. 2. In this outcome the wife has to undertake a double shift—having to sacrifice her leisure hours and work at the office and home. Studies show that sharing of household tasks is rarely practiced even in nuclear families (COD 2004; Upadhyay 2005). By and large, gender stereotyping of household roles persists. Women accepted the practice of husbands being responsible for 'outside the house' tasks related to financial matters, while they looked after household chores despite their late nights.

2.6.3 The Mommy Track as a Cul-de-sac

Upadhya (2006) and Kelkar and Nathan (2002) argue that firms are reluctant to recruit married women with children. Apart from this there does not seem to be any other discrimination against women in the hiring process. Rather, companies like IBM, Microsoft and NIIT have been known to set targets for recruiting women. These companies also offer incentives to recruitment consultancies fulfiling such targets (NASSCOM and Deloitte 2008). It is with regard to career advancement that a difference between male and female worker emerges, resulting in the clustering of women in low-level areas with lower levels of pay and with limited opportunities for growth (COD 2004; ILO 2004; Rothboeck et al. 2001; Upadhya 2006; Wirth 2001).

A major reason why women advance less slowly than male workers in general is their 'inability' to work as long as their male counterparts because of social restrictions on mobility and greater share of household responsibilities. The software sector, for instance, boasts of flexible hours. In reality, companies have core work hours corresponding to the office time of their (offshore) clients. Coupled with the individualisation of work and the need to meet over-ambitious project deadlines (Upadhya 2006), this typically results in long hours of about 14 h of work per day. In many cases, work continues over night. This is a major problem for women workers because of social disapproval, objection from families, domestic responsibilities and security-related issues involved in returning late at night (Upadhya 2006; Mitter 1995). The problem is more serious in some Business Process Outsourcing sectors, like medical transcription and call centres where work is organised in shifts. The disruption of biological clock by atypical work hours, coupled with the highly controlled and monitored work regime, leads to stress and burn out.

While such pressures operate on both male and female workers, domestic responsibilities impose additional stress on the women workers. As discussed earlier, women, even in nuclear families, have been found to bear the full responsibility for cooking, washing, cleaning, grocery shopping and childcare

(COD 2004).[8] Hence they find it difficult to combine the challenges of a demanding career with domestic well-being and social norms (Mitter 1995; Soriyan and Aina 1991). Women workers, therefore, typically work shorter hours than male workers (Rothboeck et al. 2001), and are unable to participate in the informal knowledge networks that are important for upward mobility (COD 2004; Upadhya 2006). As a result, women workers generally have limited access to the informal knowledge networks important for upward mobility (Upadhya 2007). The limited access of women workers to networks within the office is not only because they have to return home early, but also owing to men workers feeling uneasy socially interacting with their women colleagues (COD 2004).

It has been observed that women workers in the IT sector postpone marriage and having children. Many women workers are often reluctant to accept on-site (particularly offshore) assignments and travel abroad because of family reasons (Ramsay and McCorduck 2005). For instance, 63 % of women workers surveyed did not accept offshore assignments (COD 2004).

A significant proportion of women workers also leave, being unable to bear the pressure of balancing their responsibilities as a worker and mother (COD 2004; Upadhya 2006). Further, aspirations of wives are often subordinate to the career of the husband—women workers generally resign when their husbands shift to other cities (COD 2004).

Overall, the early optimism about the impact of emergence of the IT sector on women's employment and agency seems to have been misplaced. As Mies (1986) predicted, global capitalism simply interacted with local patriarchy. The result was the superimposing of class over gender, relegating women to the position of tools to satisfy consumerism and work needs of a male-dominated society. In short, regional studies of women workers had shown that the IT revolution was a false dawn. But the literature only examines the decisions and its impact on the career growth of respondents—they fail to explore the processes underlying the decision-making. In particular, do respondents have any alternative—are they forced to take these decisions, or are they carefully balancing different conflicting goals; are the women themselves happy with their content status, or is their aspirations continuously repressed? These issues are explored in the next two chapters.

2.7 Summing Up

To sum up, the works of the early feminist writers reviewed here have successfully established issues like gender, empowerment and the relationship between gender and work not only as important research areas but as issues of major concern to society and policy makers. For instance, Mies (1980) examined how capitalism

---

[8] Women workers living in joint families cope better, while parents of unmarried women generally undertake household tasks.

and patriarchy are interlinked and mutually reinforce each other to subordinate women workers to a perpetually inferior position. But, the pessimistic conclusions of the Marxist school of writers, without any clear indication on how to use participation in the labour market as a means for emancipation and empowerment of women, meant that feminism was leading towards a cul-de-sac. It was necessary to emerge out of the shadows of such pessimism and identify the windows of opportunity that are opening up for women from different socio-economic backgrounds.

In the next chapter, we will start with a criticism of the Marxist feminist writers and identify the shortcomings of their studies. Arguing in favour of a more subtle and dynamic approach towards gender relations, we will review the newly emerging feminist works that seek to explore how marginalised women adopt strategies to cope with the pressures of patriarchy to carve out some space to exercise their agency. This will be used as the basis to set out the framework employed in this study.

References

Arizpe, L., & Arande, J. (1981). The comparative advantages of women's disadvantages: Women workers in the strawberry export agribusiness in Mexico. *Signs, 7*, 455–473.

Badgett, M., Lee, V., & Folbre, N. (2001). Gender norms and economic outcomes. In M. F. Loutfi (Ed.), *Women, gender and work: What is equality, and how do we get there?* (pp. 327–341). Geneva: ILO.

Banerjee, N. (1985). *Women workers in the unorganized sector: The Calcutta experience.* Hyderabad: Sangam Books Pvt Ltd.

Banerjee, N. (1991). *Indian women in a changing industrial scenario.* New Delhi: Sage Publishers.

Banerjee, N. (1992). Poverty, work and gender in urban India. (Occasional Paper No. 133). Kolkata: Centre for Studies in Social Sciences.

Barajas, E., Maria del Rosío, & Yalán, M. S. (1995). Rotación de personal en la industria maquiladora de Tijuana: Mujeres y condiciónes de vida. In S. Gonzalvez, O. Ruiz & O. Woo (Eds.), *Mujeres, migracion y maquila en la frontera norte.* Tinjuana: El Colegio de la Frontera Norte.

Bell, D. (1981). Women's business is hard work: Central Australian aboriginal women's love rituals. *Signs, 7*(2), 314–337.

Brannon, J. T., & Lucker, G. W. (1990). The impact of Mexico's economic crisis on the demographic composition of the maquiladora labour force. *Journal of Borderland Studies, 4*, 39–70.

Braunstein, E., & Folbre N. (1999). To honour or obey: Efficiency, equity and patriarchal property rights. Unpublished manuscript. Armherst, MA: Department of Economics, University of Massachusets.

Braverman, H. (1974). *Labour and monopoly capital.* New York: Monthly Review Press.

Carnoy, M. (2001). The family, flexible work and social cohesion at risk. In: M. F. Loutfi (Ed.), *Women, Gender and Work: What is equality, and how do we get there?* (pp. 305–325). Geneva: ILO.

Centre for Organization Development. (2004). *Final report on women in information technology.* Report submitted to Department of Women and Child, Ministry of Human Resource Development, Government of India, Hyderabad.

Clarke, A., & Sekher, T. V. (2007). Can career-minded young women reverse gender discrimination? A view from Bangalore's high tech sector. *Gender, Technology and Development, 11*(3), 285–319.

Cooper, Cary, & Davidson, Marilyn. (1982). *High pressure: Working lives of women managers.* London: Walter Fontana.

Coyle, A. (1989). Women in management: A suitable case for treatment? *Feminist Review, 31*(Spring), 117–125.

Crouter, A. C. (1984). Spillover from family to work: The neglected side of the work-family interface. *Human Relations, 37*(6), 425–442.

Dilworth, J. E. L. (2004). Predictors of negative spillover from family to work. *Journal of Family Issues, 3*(25), 241–261.

Elson, D., & Pearson, R. (1981). Nimble fingers make cheap workers: An analysis of women's employment in third world export manufacturing, *Feminist Review, 7(Spring)*, 87–107.

England, P., & Folbre, N. (1999). The costs of caring. *Annals of the American Academy of Political and Social Science, 561*, 39–51.

Fernandez Kelley, M. P. (1981). Development and the sexual division of labour. *Signs, 7*(2), 268–278.

Fernandez Kelley, M. P. (1983). *For we are sold, I and my people: Women and industry in Mexico's frontier.* Albany: State University of New York Press.

Folbre, N. (1994). *Who pays for the kids? Gender and the structures of constraint.* New York: Routledge.

Folbre, N., & Weisskopf, T. E. (1998). Did Father know best? Families, markets and the supply of caring labor. In A. Ben-Ner & L. Putterman (Eds.), *Economics, values and organization* (pp. 171–205). New York: Cambridge University Press.

Frobel, F., Heinrich, J., & Kreye, O. (1979). *The new international division of labour.* Cambridge: Cambridge University Press.

Fussel, E. (2000). Making labour flexible: The recomposition of Tijuana's maquiladora female labour force. *Feminist Economics, 6*(3), 59–70.

Gaio, F. J. (1995). Women in software programming: the experience of Brazil. In S. Mitter & S. Rowbotham (Eds.), *Women encounter technology: Changing patterns of employment in the third world* (pp. 205–232). New York: Routledge.

Greenhaus, J. H., & Beutell, N. J. (1985). Sources of conflict between work and family roles. *The Academy of Management Review, 10*(1), 76–88.

Grossman, R. (1979) Women's place in the integrated circuit. *Southeast Asia chronicle and Pacific review (joint issue), 66/9*(5), 2–17.

International Labour Organization. (2004). *Breaking through the glass ceiling: Women in management, 2004 update.* Geneva: International Labour Organization.

Jain, D., & Banerjee, N. (Eds.) (1985). *Tyranny of the household.* Shakti Books, Delhi.

Jones, G. (2007). Delayed marriage and very low fertility in Pacific Asia, *Population Development Review, 33*(3), 453–478.

Joshi, H. (1990). The cash opportunity cost of childbearing: An approach to estimation using British evidence. *Population Studies, 44*(1), 161–183.

Joshi, H. (1998). The opportunity costs of childbearing: More than mothers' business. *Journal of Population Economics, 11*(2), 41–60.

Kelkar, G., & Nathan, D. (2002). Gender relations and technological change in Asia. *Current Sociology, 50*(3), 427–441.

Koggel, C. M. (2003). Globalization and women's paid work: Expanding freedom? *Feminist Economics, 9*(2–3), 163–183.

Lee, Y.-J. (2006). Risk factors in the rapidly rising incidence of divorce in Korea, *Asian Population Studies, 2*(2), 113–131.

Lim, L. Y. C. (1978) *Women workers in multinational corporations: The case of the electronics industry in Malaysia and Singapore.* Michigan Occasional Paper No. 9, Women Studies Program. Ann Arbor: University of Michigan.

Marx, K. (1976). *Capital* (Vol. I). Hammondsworth: Penguin Books.

Mies, M. (1980). *Indian women and patriarchy*. New Delhi: Concept Publishing House.

Mies, M. (1986). *Patriarchy and accumulation on a world scale*. Zed Press: London.

Mitter, S. (1995). Information technology and working women's demand. In S. Mitter & S. Rowbotham (Eds.), *Women encounter technology: changing patterns of employment in the third world* (pp. 19–43). New York: Routledge.

Mitter, S., & Rowbotham, S. (Eds.). (1995). *Women encounter technology: Changing patterns of employment in the third world*. New York: Routledge.

NASSCOM and Deloitte. (2008). *Indian IT/ITES industry: Impacting Indian economy and society 2007–2008*. New Delhi: NASSCOM.

Phillips, A., & Taylor, B. (1980). Sex and skill: Notes towards a feminist economics. *Feminist Review, 6*, 79–88.

Pleck, J. H. (1977). The work-family role system. *Social Problems, 24*, 417–427.

Poonacha, V., & Rajan, P. (1996). Women, telework and development, In Sasikumar and Ramani (Eds.), *Workshop Report: Telework and Development*, Mumbai: NCST.

Ramsey, N. & McCorduck, P. (2005). *Where are the Women in Information Technology?*. Report prepared by Anita Borg. Boulder: Institute for Women and Technology for National Center for and Information Technology, University of Colarado.

Rothboeck, S., Vijaybhaskar, M., & Gayatri, V. (2001). *Labor in the Indian economy: The case of the Indian software labour market*. New Delhi: ILO.

Safa, H. (1981). Runaway shops and female employment. *Signs, 7*(2), 418–433.

Schwartz, Felice N. (1989). Management women and the new facts of life. *Harvard Business Journal, 67*(1), 65–76.

Sen, A. K. (1999). *Development as freedom*. New York: Anchor Books.

Shanker, D. (2008). Gender relations in IT companies. *Gender, Technology and Development, 12*(2), 185–202.

Sharpston, M. (1976). International subcontracting. *World Development, 4*(4), 333–337.

Shy, O. (1995). *Industrial organization*. Cambridge, MA: The MIT Press.

Sklair, L. (1993). *Assembling for development: The maquila industry in Mexico and the United States* (2nd ed.). San Diego, CA: Centre for US-Mexico studies, University of California.

Sokoloff, N. (1980). *Between money and love*. New York: Praeger.

Soriyan, B., & Aina, B. (1991). Women's work and challenges of computerisation: The Nigeria case: Understanding and overcoming bias in work and education. In I. V. Erikson, et al. (Eds.), *Women, work and computerization*. Amsterdam: North Holland.

Standing, G. (1999). Global feminization through flexible labour: A theme revisited, *World Development, 27*(3), 583–602.

Sümer, S., Smithson, J., Maria das Dores Guerreiro, & Granlund, L. (2008) Becoming working mothers: Reconciling work and family at three particular workplaces in Norway, the UK, and Portugal. *Community, Work & Family, 11*(4), 365–384.

Tiano, S. (1994). *Patriarchy on the line: Labour, gender and ideology in the Mexican Maquila Industry*. Philadelphia: Temple University Press.

Ullmann-Margalit, E. (1977). *The emergence of norms*. Clarendon Press: Oxford.

Upadhya, C. (2005). Gender issues in the Indian software outsourcing industry. In A. Gurumurthy, P. J. Singh, A. Mundkur, & M. Swamy (Eds.), *Gender in the information society: Emerging issues* (pp. 74–84). New Delhi: UNDP-AIDP & Elsevier.

Upadhya, C. (2007). Employment, exclusion and 'merit' in the Indian IT Industry. *Economic & Political Weekly*, pp. 1863–1868.

Van Waas, M. (1981). *The multinationals strategy for labour*. Unpublished doctoral dissertation, Stanford, CA: Stanford University Press.

Vernon, R. (1966). International investment and international trade in the product cycle. *Quarterly Journal of Economics, 80*(2), 190–207.

Waldfogel, J. (1997). The effects of children on women's wages. *American Sociological Review, 62*(2), 83–106.

Wirth, L. (2001). *Breaking through the glass ceiling: Women in management*. Geneva: International Labour Organization.
Young, G. (1984). Women, development and human rights: Issues in integrated transnational production. *The Journal of Applied Behavioural Science, 20*(4), 383–401.
Young, M., & Willmott, P. (1973). *The symmetrical family*. London: Routledge.

Chapter 3
Women and Work: Towards an Alternative Approach

Abstract This chapter argues that the pessimistic conclusions of the Marxist school of writers were leading feminism towards a dead end. It identifies the shortcomings of the Marxist feminist writers, and reviews the newly emerging body of feminist work, which explores how marginalised women adopt means and strategies of resistance—starting from demonic possession and mass hysteria to militant unionism—to cope with the pressures of patriarchy and carve out some space to exercise their agency. This chapter integrates this literature along with the work of economist Herbert Simon and of sociologist Cynthia Hakim to establish the framework of this study. We argue that women test the limits that a patriarchal society sets to their agency through continual negotiation and bargaining, attempting to attain a more or less satisfactory balance between multiple conflicting goals (satisficing), rather than maximising. This evolutionary process often enables women to improve their agency in a phased manner.

Keywords Satisficing · Negotiation · Resistance

3.1 Introduction

The historical coincidence of two novel trends—of growing interest in women's changing roles worldwide and the expansion of export-based manufacturing units—had attracted the attention of researchers, particular feminist researchers, to the condition of women workers in these export-based industries. The dependency theory that was emerging at that time facilitated the interpretation of the limited data that was available to enable scholars to launch a powerful critique of the new form of capitalism. The literature has made important contributions to the understanding of why participation in paid work by itself fails to empower women and increase their agency. It also throws valuable insight into how market forces interact with socio-cultural features of the society and utilises patriarchal norms to exploit women workers. These works are a useful starting point to the issue of women workers.

Z. Husain and M. Dutta, *Women in Kolkata's IT Sector*,   49
SpringerBriefs in Sociology, DOI: 10.1007/978-81-322-1593-6_3,
© The Author(s) 2014

Unfortunately, critics argue, the grounding of the literature in dependency theory coloured the interpretation of the data. Dependency theory refers to a body of work that originated in the writings of Raul Prebisch and Hans W. Singer, and was continued by scholars like Paul Baran, A. G. Frank, Celso Furtado and Paul Sweezy. It argues that resources flow from a 'periphery' of poor and underdeveloped states to a 'core' of wealthy states, enriching the latter at the expense of the former. It is a central contention of dependency theory that poor states are impoverished and rich ones enriched by the way poor states are integrated into the 'world system'. As corollary to impoverishment of nations, the theory created the stereotype of 'poverty-stricken Third World women suffering from low wages, wretched working conditions and ruthless exploitation by multinationals located in export-processing free trade zones in Asia and Latin America' (Lim 1990, p. 191).

In particular, Lim argues, the literature suffers from certain methodological flaws that have reduced the analytical significance and policy relevance of its findings. These defects are discussed below.

3.2 Limitations of the Marxist Literature

3.2.1 Static Ahistorical Approach

The literature on women workers in export-based industries overlooks the dynamism of the industries and the economies (Lim 1988) to adopt a static ahistorical approach to the problem. The feminist literature uses observations from export-based industries in their infancy. At this point of time, labour market were slack, workers lacked experience and skills but had unrealistic expectations about working conditions and were yet to adjust to the regimented factory life. The low wages earned by women workers may be justified on the grounds that workers were earning 'probationary' wages. On the other hand, foreign employers were still learning to manage workforce under different cultural and regulatory conditions. Studies from the initial phase of the export-based industries have been generalised without compunction as if they represent a typical or representative situation. Over time, many of these conditions are smoothened out, as wages rise, working conditions and worker–management relations improve and workers themselves become attuned to unfamiliar working conditions. Lim cites the substantial decrease in outbreaks of mass hysteria among women workers employed in export-based factories in Singapore and Malaysia—ostensibly due to possession by spirits, but possibly due to conflict between cultural and modern gender identities—as factory employment became widespread and entrenched.

The lack of a dynamic historical approach seriously distorts perspectives on this issue. Thus, findings from the mid-1970s are still quoted as authoritative and reflective of present conditions (Fuentes and Ehrenreich 1983; Mies 1986; Ward 1986), overlooking the enormous changes that have occurred in this sector between the 1970s and 1980s (Lim 1988).

3.2.2 *Comparison with Developed Countries*

The choice of an appropriate comparative standard to evaluate working conditions in export-based units is another major flaw. Studies generally compare wages and other working conditions in female intensive export-based firms with those prevailing in developed countries. This does not permit evaluation of whether entry of multi-national companies (MNCs) has raised levels of income and standard of living in developing countries. The appropriate control group is workers in other industries or occupations, or those who are unemployed. Lim points out:

> In most developing countries, the structure of the economy does not provide many modern wage jobs for women, most of whom are concentrated in inferior employment in farming, domestic services, and the informal sector. Modern factory jobs, whether in the export or domestic sector, are thus much desired (Lim 1990, p. 105).

Lim (1990) admits that the 'wages earned by women workers in these (export-based manufacturing) industries are typically lower than average wages for the manufacturing sector as a whole' (108), but argues that this is economically justified on several counts:

> Export industries are typically of more recent vintage than the import substituting industries that dominate most Third World manufacturing sectors; thus their workers are younger, have less seniority and receive lower wages. Export industries are also usually labour-intensive and must be competitive in the world market; they consequently can afford to pay less than tariff-protected, monopolistic, often capital-intensive and high-profile (if inefficient) industries supplying the domestic market, which can always raise prices to cover high wages. The preponderance of female workers in export industries also means a lower average wage in these industries than in the predominantly male-intensive domestic market industries; this is because domestic role conflicts mean that women usually have a much shorter working life and thus less experienced, less training, less seniority, and lower productivity and wage than male workers. Sex and age discrimination by employers which affects women who seek to re-enter the labour force after rearing children, and a sometimes lower rate of unionization due to higher turn-over and weaker commitment to the labour force contribute to a lower wage for female workers (Lim 1990, p. 108).

But, even though wages are lower in export industries than in other manufacturing sectors, such wages are higher than in other sectors of the economy—higher than earnings in agriculture, service sector and in the informal economy. Women workers in the Mexican maquiladoras, for instance, earned at least the minimum legal wage despite the high rate of unemployment prevailing in the 1970s and 1980s (about 40 %). Similarly, in countries like Bangkok and Manila, where only one out of every tenth worker gets the minimum legal wage, all women working in MNCs are paid the minimum wage. This is because the industrial sector is subject to more regulations, thereby affording some degree of protection to the workers. As a result, although conditions are inferior compared to developed countries, women workers can earn higher income by working for shorter hours in better conditions than in the informal, household and agricultural sectors.

3.2.3 Use of Ethnographic Approach

Another methodological flaw of the existing literature is the tendency to attribute all the observed impacts of women's analysis export factory employment in developing countries to the drive for 'super-profits of MNCs' by 'super-exploiting' Southeast Asian labour. Instead of adopting a multivariate approach to causality that would be more appropriate to underpin the causes of low wages and poor working conditions, researchers base their conclusions on selective, anecdotal accounts focusing on extreme situations. This approach has created a stereotyped image of MNCs from developed countries located in export-processing zones in developing countries. According to this image, MNCs recruit young unmarried women and ruthlessly exploit them by forcing them to work in harsh, unhygienic factory conditions and paying them below subsistence wages. Women get exhausted easily; this, along with social pressure to withdraw from the labour market to marry and bear children, results in a high turn-over. Simultaneously, they are exploited by their families who appropriate their wages without according them with corresponding status and power within the household.

The early feminist writings overlook the fact that MNCs do not constitute the majority of employers; nor are most of the local firms located in the export-oriented sector. Further, there is considerable diversity in age, marital status and educational level of women workers across countries. In countries like Thailand and Philippines, where a large rural surplus labour implies that cheap childcare services are available and where local customs traditionally recognise the independence of women, older women not only continue to work after marriage but even enter employment.

Feminist research also overlooks the economic background of women workers in export industries. They do not always come from poor backgrounds and are not always rural migrants. In the Asian Newly Industrialized Countries (NICs) of Taiwan, Singapore, Hong Kong and South Korea, for instance, a large proportion of women workers are located in either prosperous urban areas, or in their hinterlands. Some of them are forced to work to avoid destitution, but quite a few do so to improve their living standards. Foo and Lim (1987) shows that some of these women are accorded substantial respect for their economic contribution; this allows them greater say within the household sphere, indicating an increase in agency.

Ultimately, Lim (1990) argues, contextual conditions determine the impact of employment in export industries on welfare and agency of the women workers. In general, women workers are best off in Asian NICs, the countries most heavily involved in export manufacturing and over a longer duration. In these countries, full employment conditions imply that workers have greater bargaining power. Firms invest in technology to increase the minimum skill levels required. This intensifies competition for labour, enabling workers to demand high wages and better working conditions. On the other hand, conditions are worst in very poor countries where there are relatively few export factories and where unemployment rates are high, depressing wages and reducing the supply-side competition for labour.

3.2.4 Unionisation and Other Forms of Labour Resistance

Feminist studies of women workers in export-based industries report the docility of women workers and the lack of a resistance strategy (Bose and Acosta-Belen 1995; Elson and Pearson 1981; Hossfield 1990). They argue that it is precisely these traits that encourage their recruitment into the workforce in these sectors. Gallin (1990) argues that the influence of patriarchy, repressive labour policies adopted in NICs and a tendency to identify with the management (rather than their male colleagues) as factors that mute class consciousness. This ignores the considerable and ingenuous unique form of labour resistance used by women workers in export industries in south-east Asia.

A very mild form of protest is the practice of mimicking and ridiculing male supervisors in their absence. A very unusual form of protest in the semi-conductor industry is reported by Ackerman and Lee (1981), Lin (1986) and Ong (1988) in the form of spirit possession. Although women workers are normally very docile and cooperative, they suddenly start screaming with rage and shouting in the workplace, displaying violent convulsions, mumbling incoherently and displaying aggressive behaviour. Sometimes, the women become unconscious. Attempts at restraint by male supervisors are resisted with abnormal strength. Such attacks occur spontaneously, especially in the assembly and sewing departments where women workers are found. Only women are possessed. When one worker gets possessed, her behaviour frightens others; these workers are often unable to continue working and have to be send back home. Subsequently, the hysteria attack spreads like a contagion with other workers also being possessed. In 1978, 120 women working in a US factory in Sungai Way, Malaysia, were affected; the problem assumed such proportions that production had to be shut down for 3 days (Ong 1988). Ackerman and Lee (1981) report more than 40 outbreaks of such forms of mass hysteria in the Kota Selatan factory in Malaysia between April 1977 and July 1978.

Such attacks have been interpreted as 'thinly disguised protests against the dominant sex' (Lewis 1971, p. 31). Sabbah (1984) treats such behaviour as external manifestations of the guilt produced by invasion of women into economic spaces—particularly given the gendered nature of production process and its supervision. Such behaviour is considered to be equivalent to a form of erotic aggression transgressing Islamic codes of morality. This explains why women workers in a Japanese factory, where movement to toilets—even during menses— was monitored by male supervisors, had visions of spirits involving sanitary napkins. Ong remarks that such visions were manifestations of 'intense guilt (and repressed desire), and the felt need to be on guard against violation by the male management staff' (1981: 34).

Interestingly, the women workers are treated as innocent and are never punished. Even those workers who are possessed repeatedly are treated sympathetically and absolved of any blame. Although the management considers such possession as superstition, they feel that such hysteria is unmotivated and involuntary (Ackerman and Lee 1981). The victims, on the other hand, expressed strong grievances against the management. They complained about the low wages, the decision to withhold commission, strict leave rules and fear of male production supervisors. This leads Ong to interpret such hysteria as 'a traditional way of rebelling against authority without punishment' (1988: 33). It would explain why spirits possess women in the workplace and why they are disclosed through microscopes used in semi-conductor industries. It also explains the belief that the hum of factory production and release of effluents disturb the graveyard spirits, leading to ghostly reprisals against the factories.

Apart from such unusual forms of protest, women workers have also been reported to adopt more traditional means of resistance. Workers who were possessed report that their colleagues 'covertly cooperated to reduce production output to spite the management' (Ackerman and Lee 1981, p. 795). The active unionism and strikes organised by women workers in South Korea in the 1970s and 1980s to protest against the poor pay and working conditions is a marked contrast to the labour inactivity displayed by their male colleagues (Mikyoung 2003). The intensity and duration of some of these movements,[1] as well as the violence with which they had to be repressed, is inconsistent with the stereotype of docile cooperative women workers, rigidly bound by patriarchal norms and without any class consciousness.

3.2.5 Heterogeneity Within Workforce

Another problem with the early phase of feminist literature is that it tends to view women workers as a homogeneous category, neglecting considerable differences in their socioeconomic, cultural and demographic background. This results in a failure to analyse how the local context mediates the impact of involving women in the labour market.

For instance, in Asian NICs and in Malaysia, the economy is characterised by high wages and full employment. On one hand, high wages reduces the economic necessity of women working; on the other hand, full employment and the consequent absence of a reserve labour surplus implies that childcare services are not readily available. Social norms, too, act as a bar to married women working. This has reduced the average age of women workers in these countries.

In Thailand and Philippines, in contrast, average male income is low and unemployment levels high. This creates a pressure for women to enter the job market. The entry of women into the labour market is facilitated by the availability of childcare services through extended families and rural surplus labour. The social positioning of women, as independent agents, is also important. These

---

[1] For instance, the Dong-II textile strikes continued from 1976 to 1980.

forces imply that it is possible for older women to remain in employment, even after marriage and pregnancy in these countries.

Considerable variations in educational attainments of women workers are also observed between different sectors. Workers in the industries set up in the first phase of export-led industrialisation, namely textile and garments industries, were less educated. The electronics industries set up subsequently had, in contrast, higher average levels of education. One reason for this change was that the workers were recruited from a population that had become more educated with the spread of mass education. Secondly, over time, the industries employed more sophisticated technology requiring literacy and numeric knowledge.

Thus, women workers are considerably differentiated in their background. Such differences can create variations in choice of sectors and level of entry. Further, differences in socioeconomic background of women workers typically means that the expectations, norms and practices restricting and defining the choice set of the women workers may also vary. Analysing the impact of employment on welfare and agency of women will, therefore, become more complex than indicated in the uni-dimensional static studies reviewed above.

3.3 Why an Alternative Perspective?

As pointed out earlier, an important feature of the Marxist literature is its focus on women workers from low income households. Such women comprise a large section of the society. Moreover, the interaction between innate socioeconomic vulnerability of such women, coupled with gender norms increasing such vulnerability, render such studies doubly interesting and important for policy purposes. As seen, women workers in export-based units and in the informal sector were exploited in three ways:

1. Entry in low skill and low paid jobs.
2. Use as reserve labour without security of tenure. This rules out any prospects of career growth.
3. Refusal to acknowledge economic contribution of women workers. As a result, there are no major changes in their status within society or households.

Now a reasonably significant proportion of the workforce is from the high income households. In particular, the rapid structural changes in economies of developing countries has created substantial employment opportunities for educated women hailing from affluent, 'modern' and educated households, examining how entry into the labour market affects the status and agency of such women becomes an issue that may have important sociological and policy implications. NSSO (2011) reports that a substantially high per cent of women belonging to the highest monthly per capita expenditure decile group is involved in economic activities in both rural and urban areas (Fig. 3.1).

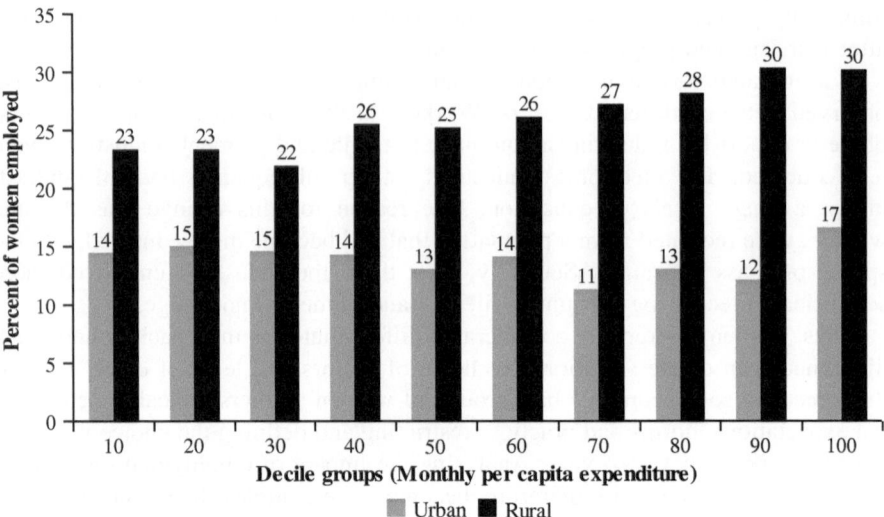

Fig. 3.1 Women employed according to usual status by decile classes on monthly per capita consumer expenditure—2009–2010. *Source* NSSO (2011, p. 81)

A sizeable section of such workers find work in highly skilled capital-intensive formalised sectors—in industries like finance, software and engineering. In such industries, the above channels of exploitation cannot operate. For instance, gender-based recruitment is not legally permitted. Similarly, the nature of job contracts in the formal sector rule out the possibility of high turn-over in labour force in tune with fluctuations in demand in world markets. The high pay of women workers, often at par with that of spouses, also means that it is difficult to ignore the economic contribution of these women.

Although, the forms of exploitation prevalent in the lower end of the labour market will not work in the top end of the labour market, this does not imply that such women are free from all types of exploitation. Rather it is the *form* of exploitation that varies. The synergistic interaction of market driven and house-hold/society driven processes simply operates in a different (often more subtle) way and has different repercussions for this category of women. Obviously, we will have new forms of exploitation.

Mies (1980) points out that, in case of role conflicts, if *both* roles are institu-tionalised, they become legitimate. This intensifies the conflict as the family cannot disqualify any of the conflicting behaviour as deviant. In case of employment, Mies continues, the economic necessity of allowing women to work has imparted a sense of de facto legitimacy to the role of women as a worker. This sets up a situation of conflict with the traditional role of woman as caregiver (Fig. 3.2).

The problem with the visualisation in Fig. 3.2 is that it fails to incorporate feedbacks in the form of changing expectations, and its impact on the evolution of

Fig. 3.2 Conflict between
roles—static view

Traditional structure of society

Traditional role as care-giver

ROLE CONFLICT

New role as worker

Economic necessity

the family. For instance, as in Fig. 3.3, the conflict between two legitimate roles may also modify expectations about each role. This brings about a gradual social change that, in turn, redefines the conflicting roles. Such changes may be facilitated by contextual changes. In the example that we are considering, for instance, factors like technological progress (making traditional household chores easier to perform) and changes in market for care services may reduce the conflict between roles. This reshapes constraints on the role of women and permits them to exercise greater autonomy in their decision-making. Given the rapid changes in lifestyle that has swept Indian society in the last two decades, we argue, this is precisely what has been happening. Therefore, unless we incorporate this process of change in our examination of the balance between work and household, our analysis will remain blinkered.

At the same time, it is not so easy to shake off the vestiges of the past. For instance, Campbell (1996) argues that habits may seek to perpetuate quasi-aspects of the traditional past. Thus, we must take into account two possibilities—contextual forces promoting agency and remnants of the past exercising constraints on the choice set. The analytical model used to describe the impact of work on women's agency has to take into account such interactions and possibilities.

For instance, the high wages in these sectors and long working hours implies that the conflict between the traditional image of Indian women as providers of

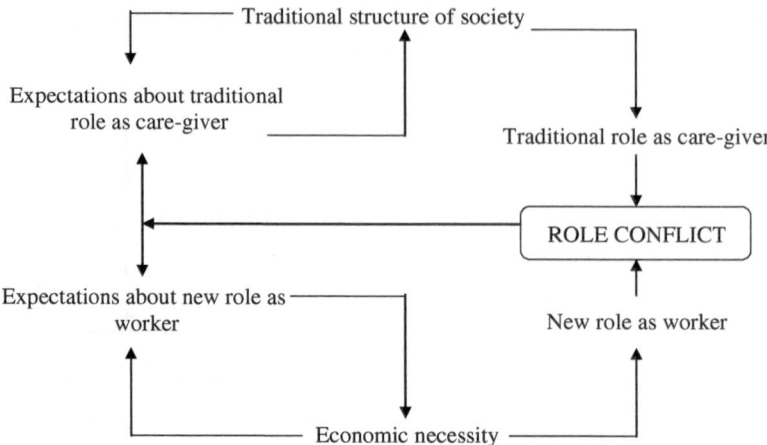

Fig. 3.3 Conflict between roles—dynamic view

care services within their family and the emerging role of the women as a dedi-
cated worker with ambitions relating to career growth will be a sharp one.
Simultaneously, the costs and benefit of maintaining traditional norms and patterns
of behaviour, too, change. The change in the context in which role conflict occurs
may either open up new windows of opportunity for the empowerment of women
or close such windows by changing the nature of exploitation to more subtle
forms.

3.4 The Emerging Feminist Literature

In the last two decades, there have been several studies undertaken by an emerging
school of feminist researchers who have highlighted how marginalised women
create space to exercise their agency in diverse situations. We briefly review their
works in this section.

3.4.1 Bargaining with Patriarchy

In recent years, feminist researchers are increasingly discarding the binary nar-
rative of women as passive and marginalised victims of a patriarchal society.
The focus has shifted to appreciating the complexities encountered by women and
the implications for agency and empowerment. Such studies continue to examine
the constraints binding women, but also explore the 'strategies of resistance,
rebellion and collective organisation they deploy in their every day lives'

(Thapan 2005, p. 24). Instead of portraying women as passive agents or victims of oppression and exploitation, such works 'emphasises the manner in which they are able to exercise their agency in the twin process of submission and assertion, simultaneously challenging the system and never being able to completely escape it' (Thapan 2005, p. 24). The important feature of such resistance, therefore, is the absence of what Takhar calls 'overt manifestation of resistance' (Takhar 2003, p. 224). Instead, women prefer to transform and subvert the dominant structures and expectations by exercising their collective and individual agency in covert ways, circumventing established norms and behavioural practices through subtle, devious means (Thapan 2005, p. 39).[2]

For instance, some feminist writers argue, women maximise resources within the patriarchal system through various strategies (Collier 1974; di Leonardo 1987; Kibria 1990). Kandiyoti (1988), for instance, suggests that the strategies adopted by women reveal the blueprint of what she calls the 'patriarchal bargain'. This bargain refers to the ways and means through which women and men negotiate and adapt to the set of rules that guide and constrain gender relations within a patriarchal society. The nation notion of bargaining with patriarchy suggests that both men and women possess resources with which they negotiate to maximise power and options within a patriarchal structure. The bargaining is obviously asymmetric—for, as long as patriarchy exists, the power and options available to women will be less than those of men in the same society (class). Nevertheless,

> … such bargains exert a powerful influence on the shaping of women's gendered subjectivity and determine the nature of gender ideology in different contexts. They also influence both the potential for and specific forms of women's active or passive resistance in the face of their oppression. Moreover, patriarchal bargains are not timeless or immutable entities, but are susceptible to historical transformations that open up new areas of struggle and renegotiation of the relation between genders" (Kandiyoti 1988, p. 275).

Feminist researchers point out that social transformation, caused through migration (Pessar 1984), modernisation (Lamphere 1987), international marriage (Patriwala and Uberoi 2008) and conflict (Behera 2006), often entails important shifts in the nature ad scope of resources available to men and women actors. A period of intense renegotiation between men and women may occur, as new bargains based on the new endowment sets are arrived at. Although such bargaining may lead to a questioning and even rejection of fundamental rules of the old social order, the fundamental characteristic of such transition in gender relations is that there need not be any no overt questioning or challenging of male authority. This allows for limited (but important) transformations in gender relations without deep shifts in men's power and authority. The reluctance to radically restructure the patriarchal society was in part due to the heavy costs of bargaining and resistance. Among other reasons were economic protection provided to the

---

[2] For instance, Riessman (2000) reports, critical and contemptuous comments directed towards childless (educated and employed) women are transformed by them as ridiculous images of the traditional order to be reported to and laughed over with similar childless women.

women by the traditional social order women and the fact that it allowed them to exercise power over younger generations.

For instance, Kibria (1990) reported that informal Vietnamese women groups played an important role in protecting status of women emigrants to USA. In case of a marital discord, for example, they interpreted the situation to show that the husband was at fault. This interpretation was based on the argument that the principle of male authority had been violated, contradicting other central familial values. Thus, women 'emerged ... as both guardians of the family and as supporters of a particular woman's interest' (Kibria 1990, p. 16).

It is clear, therefore, that we have to recognise the complex nature of women's choices and their consequences for empowerment. For instance, very often it is difficult to separate out the pressures emanating from the family to take a particular decision from a self-motivated search for greater autonomy or material progress (Thapan 2005). Moreover, instead of a frontal challenge to patriarchy, women normally adopt a cautious approach, balancing different considerations and preferring to subvert the existing order. Some of these complexities are illustrated in three different contexts in the following sub-sections.

3.4.2 Women, Migration and Work

An analysis of the motives of Malayali nurses migrating to the Gulf countries, and the impact of such movement on their autonomy, is an interesting illustration of the above arguments.

Prima facie, migration to Gulf countries is dictated by the family to maximise household welfare. The nurse is expected to send back the major part of her earnings; she is also expected to serve as node facilitating migration of other members. Migrant women also report on the family pressure to migrate, so that migration becomes a duty. Nevertheless, there are also significant components related to self-interest that influence their choice:

> I want to see the world. I want to travel. I want to learn new things. What chances do I have to do that if I become an accountant or if get any MBA? Ten years ago, they would have said 'no', and that's it, but to be a nurse is not the social handicap as it used to be. They know that there won't be any money problem for me and that I'll help, maybe, have a better marriage than the one they imagined (reported in Percot 2006, p. 171).

Most of the nurses perceive migration as a liberation which will enable them to realise their individual aspirations more easily. As Alice, one of the nurses migrating to Chicago, remarks:

> I don't want to work to pay for all the uncles and aunties of the family, for the dowries or the studies of some cousins I hardly know. I don't want to come back home just to show off with a three storey house, spending my time drinking tea with old ladies of the family while my husband will be driving everybody in his beautiful car (Percot 2006, pp. 171–172)

As Thapan (2005) points out, while it is true that the decision to migrate cannot be considered an autonomous choice of the women, the women also expect that the decision will satisfy their individual aspirations. Further, the financial independence resulting from work instils a sense of confidence in the working women. Migration provides a mean of escape from the traditional order to a society providing scope for the expansion of their individual aspirations and identities; it is abroad that they can satisfy their emerging need for autonomy. Percot observes that:

> Migrant nurses are quite conscious that by providing good economic returns to their family, they take on the traditional task of the man and never miss to point this out. All of them are rather proud of their capacity for good earnings and of their ability to open the way to migration for their spouse or other members of the family. Furthermore, this opportunity is also what gives a new and better status to any nurse (Percot 2006, p. 170).

3.4.3   Women in Transnational Families

The literature on transnational family life has received considerable attention, most of which is negative. The documenting of issues like sex trafficking, serial grooms, 'Mail Order Brides', marital violence and abuses of human dignity by emigration officers have resulted in women being portrayed as marginalised victims manipulated by their families/husbands/other (male) actors involved in such migration. Women's role in migration has generally been denigrated, so that they appear passive and secondary actors.

In contrast, the emerging feminist literature shows that migration may also lead to the 'rescripting of gender roles within the family and offer women economic security and escape from subjection and persecution, as well as enhanced autonomy and respect in both the family and community' (Palriwala and Uberoi 2008, p. 23). Del Rosario (1994), Fan and Huang (1998), Fan and Li (2002) argue that migration linked to marriage may often be the best strategy to move up the socioeconomic ladder. Kalpagam (2008) and Charsleys (2008) demonstrate that transnational marriage may be a carefully devised strategy to build up social capital for the family—with the women playing a pivotal role in creating the network for migration of other family members. As Gallo remarks, marriage is a 'traditional framework through which families can express 'modern' achievements in terms of educational, social, or geographical mobility and access to consumer goods' (2008, p. 191). There is even a sense of agency possessed by Mail Order Brides, who are quite aware of the possibility of being exploited, but discount this as a necessary cost in their cold blooded self-seeking pursuit of materialism. Of course there is an asymmetry, with daughters of women who migrate being more empowered and able to exercise greater agency in their choices and actions. Such works also show that the gains from transnational migration may be accompanied by guilt and fractured identities (Mand 2008), enriching the traditional binary narratives with layers of complexity.

3.4.4 Women in the Times of Conflict

In literature on women displaced as a result of conflict refugee, women are typically represented as poverty-stricken victims without any agency. Critics of this approach argue against simplified universal application of such theorisation. Nayanika Mookherjee (2006), for instance, argues that exclusion of the experiences of the middle class refugees and over-emphasis on poor women refugees as passive victims leads to binary narratives of agent–victim and male–female. Such binary narratives overlook the potential for adventure, romance and excitement that may be derived from conflict situations like the Bangladesh war of independence by virtue of one's class. Mookherjee's study shows how the social disturbance provided space for middle class women to express themselves and emerge out of their traditional feminine stereotype to play an active role in raising morale. Similarly, O'Kane's study of migration in the Thai-Myanmar border shows that the disruption of the social fabric by the violence of partition created a vacuum where women were cast in unfamiliar non-traditional roles in a space where public/private had become blurred (O'Kane 2006). The need for family survival in a rapidly collapsing social order enabled the marginalised migrant women to challenge established gender norms and, paradoxically, use the situation to their relative advantage. Rajasingham-Senanayake (2006) reveals how displacement, by leading to an erosion of caste ideology and practice, contributes to women's mobility and empowerment.

Such 'ambivalent empowerment' born out of loss and displacement (Rajasingham 2000) has, of course, been contested (Saigol 2000; Khattak 1995). In particular, increasing domestic violence, the guilt displayed by the women breaking traditional norms and the failure to develop cultural frameworks that will legitimise such structural transformations poses questions regarding the permanence of the empowerment displayed by the refugee women. But the sense of self-worth and identity of many of these refugees (Thiruchandran 1999), their capacity for political discourse (Thiruchandran 1999), their resistance (Saigol 2000) does provide hope for the future.

3.5 An Alternative Perspective Towards Decision-Making

The feminist literature makes an important contribution to gender studies by arguing that we should not treat the absence of resistance as an indication of passivity. Rather, they emphasise on the bargaining and negotiation carried out constantly between women and a patriarchal society—leading to a subtle subversion of the dominant male-centric society. The apparent compliance with altruistic goals imposed by the patriarchal society is often used as an instrument to satisfy individual aspirations, indicating that women are capable of utilising opportunities embedded in the local socioeconomic context and adopting strategies that reduce role conflict and ease pressure on them. This view also points out that the conflict between women in their traditional role of provider of care services and the new role of women as worker should not be conceptualised in static terms. It stresses the possibility that conflict between two legitimate roles may generate social processes that weaken patriarchal norms and modify expectations. Conflict is reduced over time, which generates positive effects on the agency of women workers. The new feminist writers, therefore, reject the conceptualisation of women as 'grateful slaves', passively accepting the bounds imposed by their families, society and the organisational structure shaping their work environment.

In line with this contention, we echo the sentiment that 'It is time to abandon the concept of women so totally formed and constrained by past patterns of economic activity and sex role stereotyping that they are unable to shape their own lives to any meaningful degree' (Hakim 1991, p. 114).

In this chapter, based on the works of the new feminist writers, Hakim's work on working women and Simon's satisficing approach, we present a formal approach to the issue of working women. Starting from the scheme presented earlier (Fig. 3.3), we argue that the entry of educated women from urban affluent households into a non-traditional growing sector has created space for them to express themselves in household decisions and exercise choices. They face constraints—of which the need to balance work and household is a major concern. In this section, we argue that such balancing may be incorporated into a *satisficing* model of decision-making.

3.5.1 Theories of Social Constraints and Agency

In the 1990s Cynthia Hakim let the cat among the feminist pigeons by arguing that:

> We must stop presenting women as 'victims', or as undifferentiated mass of mindless zombies whose every move is determined by other actors and social forces ... Women are responsible adults, who make real choices and are the real authors and agents of their own lives. Some women choose to be home-centred, with work as a secondary activity. Some women choose to be career-centred, with domestic activities a secondary consideration (Hakim 1996a, p. 186).

Based upon observed polarisation of women's employment between full-time and part-time employment, Hakim (1991, 1995, 1996a, b) claimed that there are basically two kinds of women distinguished by their orientation towards work. One group has a long-term commitment towards the family, while the commitment of the other group is towards her career—with an intermediary group drifting between the two, and wanting both.[3] The former group comprises primarily

---

[3] 'A great many women 'hang loose' and refuse to choose fixed objectives, drifting with events and opportunities as they arise, pretending they can keep all their options open by refusing to close the door on any of them' (Hakim 1996b, p. 208).

homemakers and nurturers, holding part-time jobs that give them sufficient freedom to fulfil their household duties. The second group comprises careerist women, who resemble men workers with respect to their continuity of participation in the workforce over their working life. The careerist group of women takes advantage of the introduction of household gadgets to facilitate household tasks, depends on reliable contraceptive methods to plan (or even avoid) pregnancy and utilises available childcare services to reduce the cost of withdrawal from the labour force.

The stable commitment of each of these two groups is not forced upon them, but is made deliberately and is shaped, Hakim argues, by their early adulthood and family environment. Thus, they are not 'forced' into their roles as secondary workers and primary home makers. Rather their choice is made on the basis of values and orientations developed before entry into the labour market (viz. preferences), and their behaviour moulded by the interaction of their preferences with the economic consequences of their action.

Hakim ruffled the feathers of quite a few feminist sociologists. They were quick to draw attention to the loopholes of her theory. Initial criticism stressed the static nature of her theories (Bruegel 1996) and undue emphasis on attitudes and family orientation (Ginn et al. 1996). Other sociologists were more constructive, attempting to combine the structure of society and agency of the actor. Continental sociologists pointed out that post-War changes in work, education and family structure force/allow people to make their own choice and carve out their destiny in an increasingly complex world (Beck 1992; Buchman 1989). Bates and Risebrough (1993) stressed the disintegrative effect of competition for scarce resources on social bonds and the creation of individual competitive identities. Others focus on the adaptive nature of actors. Chisholm and Du-Bois Reymond (1993) highlighted the tendency of British teenagers to accommodate their aspirations to structural realities. Similarly, Roberts (1993) noted that the youth do not appear to be moving passively towards societal goals/destinations, but try to carve out a path for themselves towards individual goals, in the face of multiple obstacles.

Therefore, instead of structural determination, we have what Roberts (1993) calls, 'structured individuation'—actors have individual aspirations and goals, but the characteristics of their structural locations determine their ability to realise such targets. Faced with obstacles, actors adapt aspirations; but, given the complexity of situational forces and individual nature of targets, each individual has a virtually unique outcome (Proctor and Padefield 1998). It is in this context that the 'satisficing' approach (Simon 1955) becomes relevant.

3.5.2 Satisficing Approach

The theory of satisficing was developed by Herbert Simon (1955, 1956) in response to the perceived limitations of the economic theory of rationality. In particular, Simon pointed out, rationality theory assumes knowledge of the relevant aspects of his environment which, if not absolutely complete, is at least impressively clear and voluminous. He is assumed also to have a well-organized and stable system of preferences, and a skill in computation that enables him to calculate, for the alternative courses of action that are available to him, which of these will permit him to reach the highest attainable point on his preference scale (Simon 1955, p. 99).

Simon argues that the extent of information and degree of computational skill required on the part of the agent is far in excess of what is possessed by the agent in reality. Moreover, the assumption that the agent can accurately predict the outcome from each and every action—leaving no room for unanticipated consequences—is also unrealistic. In reality, actual decision-making occurs in a far more simplified setting than conceived under rationality theory.

The foundation of Simon's theory of satisficing is that the innate ability of the agent and the environment in which the environment is situated imposes limits to the extent of information possessed by the agent or her ability to process information. This defines the *de facto* feasible zone, which is smaller than the feasible set that is nominally available to the agent, within which the agent chooses. In such a case, Simon continues, a possible decision rule is to identify a set of outcomes which is more satisfactory to the agent than her present position and try to attain one of these outcomes. This decision rule is called satisficing (Simon 1955).

Satisficing is an alternative to optimisation for cases where there are multiple and competitive objectives and in which one gives up the idea of obtaining the 'best' solution (Simon 1955). In this approach, the actor sets lower bounds for the various objectives that, if attained, will be satisfactory, or 'good enough', and then seeks a solution that will exceed these bounds. The satisficer's philosophy is that in the real world there are far too many uncertainties and conflicts in values thereby negating the hope of obtaining a true optimisation. Hence it is more sensible to set out to improve on one's current situation and do 'well enough'.

Two points may be noted at this junction. First, this outcome, lying within the de facto feasible set, may be inferior to points within the complete feasible set available to the agent. But, the lack of information, ability to process information or predictive ability leads to a failure to identify this point as lying within the de facto feasible set. Second, if the agent has more information, is skilled in information processing or has strong predictive powers, the agent will have a wider de facto feasible set, so that she can move closer to the 'optimising' point.

3.5.3 Satisficing Approach to Education, Work and Household

Let us now examine how satisficing explains the work–household balance, given that women prefer patriarchal bargaining and covert subversion of the dominant behavioural patterns and norms to overt confrontation.

We start from a situation where women have low levels of entitlements and endowments, measured in terms of education, ownership of financial resources and access to the labour market. Obviously, this will result in low levels of capability and absence of women's freedom to act. In terms of the satisficing theory, such constraints will also limit the de facto feasible set. For instance, 'overthrowing' patriarchy will be difficult not only in terms of lack of sufficient power of the women, but also because of the uncertain gains from such an action. Patriarchy, for all its exploitation, also offers some benefits to women—economic security, means to tide over crisis,[4] ability to enjoy power in other domain.[5]

In terms of Fig. 3.4, women have two objectives—seeking greater empowerment through education and employment, or submitting overtly to patriarchy and devoting herself to household work. The optimum position (S*) is outside the feasible set of women and may be difficult to attain, either because of internalised norms, uncertain effects and high costs of resisting patriarchy, or other such reasons. Given the constraints on possible action and lack of predictive behaviour, women can only identify a possible zone with outcomes more satisfactory to the current one (H_0). This zone is defined by minimum levels of the two targets—education/employment ($E\&E_1$) and household work (HW_1)—that the woman seeks to ensure. The area considered by the woman to be satisfactory is given to the right of H, between the two lines $E\&E_1$ and HW_1 (North-east quadrant, labelled as Satisfactory zone). The feminist literature, reviewed in this chapter, suggests that women will embark on a process of patriarchal bargaining, sounding out the limits to their current agency and move to a point like S_0, which is better than the current position. If society and individual circumstances permit such a movement, then this would constitute an exercise in agency on the part of the woman. Such covert exercise has the advantage that it will subvert the existing norms and behavioural practices, without threatening social stability, so that currently unacceptable patterns of behaviour by women will become acceptable over time. An example is given by Seymour (1999):

> Her (Gitali) father opposed dance for a girl but her mother, who loves music, was supportive and allowed Gitali to study dance secretly. After some years, her father saw her perform in a dance recital and changed his mind. "He could take pride in me", she says (Seymour 1999, p. 236).

The attainment of S_0 in the first period sets the foundation for a dynamic process of negotiation with relaxation of the constraints in each 'round'—partly as a result of social change due to the subverting of social norms by women and partly as a result of increases in entitlements and endowments of women. Consequently, the set of de facto satisfactory outcomes will expand (so that $E\&E_1$ and HW_1 become $E\&E_2$ and HW_2, respectively)—so that women have greater agency

---

[4] For instance, widows are supposed to be provided support by male members (Seymour 1999, p. 111). Although such help is not always forthcoming, the possibility of means of assistance being available will act as a disincentive to resistance against patriarchy, give the marginalised position of women.

[5] For instance, older women can dominate younger women and children; women with male children can dominate unmarred or childless women, and so on (Kibria 1990; Seymour 1999).

Fig. 3.4 Satisficing
behaviour—first round

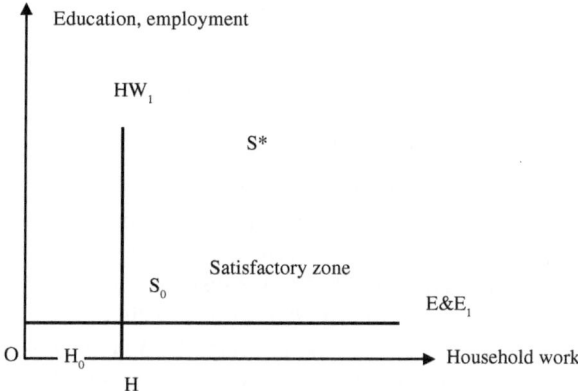

Fig. 3.5 Satisficing
behaviour—second round

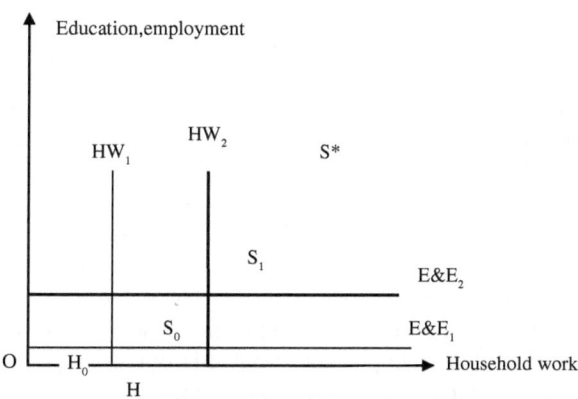

(freedom to choose). The choice situation and actual choice in the second round is depicted in Fig. 3.5. Such gradual transition allows for empowerment without threatening the social fabric and allowing time for new norms and practices maintaining social stability to emerge—'The key customs ... are indeed disappearing, but not too rapidly to allow for the building of new customs based on altered ideas, to take their place' (Minturn 1993, p. 317).

A description of such step-by-step road to empowerment is given by Seymour (1999) in her longitudinal study of transition in women's education in Bhuvaneswar from the 1960s to the 1990s. Seymour's account starts off with a grandmother who was scared off from schooling on observing her classmate getting punished. The respondent remarks, 'I only attended schooling a few days. I saw the teacher cane a child and never went back. I was self taught at home' (Seymour 1999, p. 189). But, she continues,

> I was always interested in higher education and was able to teach my own children in Oriya up to matriculation. ... I opposed my husband getting our daughters married and urged him to allow them to get highly educated first—to complete their studies. I was always interested in my daughter studying music and dance. [Their father was opposed.] I myself was interested in philosophy and aesthetics (ibid, p. 189).

The mother continues,

I was allowed to continue my education after marriage. [She had a B.A. at the time of marriage and then, after having three children, returned to graduate school to get an M.A.] I have tried to rear my own children to be independent, especially my daughter. I have done what I can for them, what I thought best at that time (ibid, pp. 189–190).

The girl, Laxmi, a postgraduate who is unmarried even at the age of 25 years, says, 'I am very free, I have free time and free choice' (ibid, p. 190).

Of course, the transition may not always be as smooth as in this family. In the case of the Tripathy family, for instance, the educational aspirations of neither the grandmother nor the mother were satisfied. The grandmother was married off at the age of seven, with the marriage being consummated 5 years later. The mother was luckier in the sense of getting 6 years of education; but, she too, was married off at the age of 15 years. In the case of the third generation only were girls educated. This was attributed to their father, but the role of the mother was also instrumental (ibid, pp. 191–192).

Such incidents indicate that, even in the same social context, individual differences may lead to equilibrium at different points in the satisfactory zone, depending upon the ability of women to exercise their agency. We can, thus, have both multiple equilibria and also alterative routes to empowerment within the satisficing zone.

In a general framework, we may conceive of social movements (like the movement for educating women in nineteenth century India), conflict, migration and other such 'shocks' disturbing the existing social order. Individual events[6] too may relax the constraints and allow the women to move to a more satisfactory point. What is important about this dynamic process of choice is that its evolutionary framework allows us to incorporate the gradualist covert strategies of resistance and subversion, reflecting constant negotiation and bargaining with a patriarchal society, ultimately enhancing agency and leading to the increase in empowerment of women.

In the present context, for instance, women have two conflicting goals—fulfilling family commitments and attending to official duties. Choice between these two options is not 'free':

Women make choices, but not under conditions of their own making. Women choose the best option that they can see, rationally, though usually with imperfect knowledge, but only within the range of options open to them. The decision as to whether to spend more time on the home or more time on paid work is a rational choice. But those choices cannot be understood outside of an understanding of the institutions and structures which construct those options (Walby 1997, p. 25).

---

[6] 'In recent years, she (Mrs. Tripathy) has assumed practically all responsibility for the family as her elderly responsibility has grown senile. *Her once distanced and respectful relationship with him has, by necessity, been transformed* (our emphasis) (Seymour 1999, p. 124).

To what extent women are able to attain each of these targets depends upon their working, family and social environment—the attitude of their matrimonial family, extent to which their husbands are supportive, attitude of colleagues and superiors, presence of external support and other factors specific to the situation.

In such situations, women are not able to maximise their welfare by choosing the best outcome, but have to embark on a negotiation process with their family and office. This negotiation enables them to test the structural limits on their agency; once such limits are reached, they adapt their aspirations and targets to structural realities to identify possible actions (like choice of departments, acceptance of offshore assignments, family planning, etc.) that will enable them to balance the two conflicting objectives. We may discuss this process using a diagram (Fig. 3.5). The two goals, fulfilling family commitment (particularly child care) and attending to official duties, are represented by F_i and W_i, respectively. But, while both goals are important to women, they are also competing.

Researches report that work and careers are perceived by respondents as important aspects of the lives of working women beyond basic financial needs. Kenny expresses the personal need for work in the following quote:

> The money angle (to having a job) is important, because you usually are short of money. But there are other things that are important about it too. There's the emotional side. There's the need to have other adults to talk to. There's the need for an outside life (Kenny 1978, p. 139)

Findings from a survey of employed women conducted by Murphy-Lawless et al. (2004) revealed that employment was both an expected and important feature of the lives of respondents. Respondents stated that having 'secure economic circumstances and social support in order to rear a child' was highly important to them (2004, p. 50). In order for the 'secure economic circumstances' to be achieved, respondents would have to have financial stability, usually through employment. Thus, these women viewed employment as a *prerequisite* to motherhood in many cases. Respondents also outlined the range of difficulties in negotiating reproductive choices with employment, such as how to have enough time and energy to do both, how to afford childcare as well as other expenses and how to fit motherhood in with employment demands and goals. On the other hand, the importance of motherhood in Indian society, traditionally held to be of great importance, is further underlined by the consumerism sweeping India after liberalisation. In this new market driven climate, the urban educated Indian woman is now an important consumer who, for the first time, has choices available to her. Consequently, advertising now adroitly combines both ideologies of feminism and femininity within discourses of consumerism construction of the 'New Indian Woman' in her multiple avatars of homemaker (Munshi 1998). This leads to a situation where women face multiple (here two) and conflicting goals.

Initially, agents are situated at S_0, representing socially determined minimum levels of both these two goals. It can be seen that movement to the north-east quadrant (Satisfactory Zone) increases their welfare levels. However, as Simon

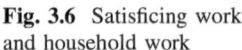

Fig. 3.6 Satisficing work and household work

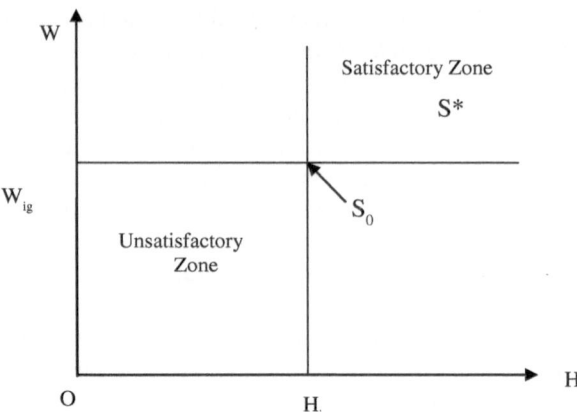

(1955) points out, agents may not be able to identify the choices/actions that will lead to outcomes like S*. In this situation, agents are not able to maximise their welfare by choosing the best outcome in the satisfactory zone. Rather they embark on a negotiation process to identify possible actions that will enable them to move to an equilibrium point in the satisfactory *zone*.

It should be recognised that this equilibrium point does not represent an equilibrium common to all respondents. Multiple equilibria are consistent with satisficing and each agent chooses her equilibrium point on the basis of individual circumstances. Furthermore, as seen in Fig. 3.6, after attaining a satisfactory point like S*, women can consolidate their gain and try to enhance their agency and empowerment through successive rounds of bargaining.

3.6 Summing Up

In this chapter, we have reviewed recent developments in the feminist literature. The limitations of the binary approach characterising initial phases of feminist writing has been acknowledged, leading to the development of an alternative approach towards gender and development. Feminist writers are challenging the notion of women as passive agents. They are increasingly documenting the different ways in which women attempt to subvert and engage in a sequential process of bargaining with the existing system. Such writings, however, fail to explain the simultaneous co-existence of (covert) resistance in some spheres alongside passivity in other spheres. In this chapter, we have set out a framework, based on the satisficing approach, which explains how women attempt to identify avenues where covert resistance is feasible and attempts to expand their capabilities along such directions. In the next two chapters, we will apply this framework to a study of women workers in the IT sector.

References

Ackerman, S. E., & Lee, R. L. M. (1981). Communications and cognitive pluralism in a spirit possession event in Malaysia. *American Ethnologist, 8*(4), 789–799.

Bates, I., & Riseborough, G. (1993). Introduction: Deepening divisions, fading solutions. In I. Bates & G. Riseborough (Eds.), *Youth and inequality* (pp. 1–3). Buckimham: Open University Press.

Beck, U. (1992). *Risk society: Towards a new modernity*. London: Sage.

Bose, C. E., & Acosta-Belen, E. (1995). Introduction. In C. E. Bose & E. Acosta-Belen (Eds.), *Women in the latin American development process* (pp. 1–14). Philadelphia: Temple University Press.

Bruegel, I. (1996). Whose myths are they anyway?: A commen'. *British Journal of Sociology, 47*(1), 175–177.

Buchmann, M. (1989). *The script of life in modern society*. London: University of Chicago Press.

Campbell, C. (1996). Detraditionalization, character and the limits to agency. In P. Heelas, S. Lash, & P. Morris (Eds.), *Detraditionalization: Critical reflections on authority and identity* (pp. 149–169). Cambridge, Massachusets: Blackwell Publishers.

Charsley, K. (2008). Vulnerable brides and 'transnational *Ghar Damads*: Gender, risk and 'adjustment' among Pakisthani marriage migrants to Britain. In R. Patriwala & P. Uberoi (Eds.), *Marriage, migration and gender* (pp. 261–285). New Delhi: Sage.

Chisholm, L., & Bois-Reymond, M Du. (1993). Youth transitions, gender and social change. *Sociology, 27*(2), 259–279.

Collier, J. (1974). Women in politics. In M. Rosaldo and L. Lamphere (Ed.) *Women, culture and society*. Stanford University Press: Palo Alto, CA.

Di Leonardo, M. (1987). The female world of cards and holidays: Women, families and the work of kinship. *Signs, 12*(3), 440–454.

Del Rosario, V. O. (1994). *Lifting the smoke: Dynamics of mail order Bride migration from the Philippines*. The Hague: Institute of Social Sciences.

Elson, D., & Pearson. (1981). "Nimble fingers make cheap workers": An analysis of women's employment in third world export manufacturing. *Feminist Review Spring, 7*, 87–107.

Fan, C. C., & Huang, Y. (1998). Waves of rural brides: Rural marriage migration in China. *Annals of the Association of American Geographers, 88*(2), 227–251.

Fan, C. C., & Li, L. (2002). Marriage and migration in transnational China: A field study of Gauzho, Western Guangdong. *Environment and Panning A, 34*(4), 619–638.

Foo, G. H. C., & Lim, L. Y. C. (1987). Poverty, ideology and women's export factory workers in Asia. In H. Afsar & B. Agarwal (Eds.), *Women and poverty*. London: Macmillan.

Fuentes, A., & Ehrenreich, B. (1983). *Women in the global factory*. Boston: Institute for New Communications Pamplet No. 3, South End Press.

Gallin, R. (1980). Women and the export industry in Taiwan: The muting of class consciousness. In K. Ward (Ed.), *Women workers and global restructuring* (pp. 179–192). Ithaca: ILR press.

Gallo, E. (2008). Unorthodox sisters: Gender relations and generational change among Malayali migrants in Italy. In R. Patriwala & P. Uberoi (Eds.), *Marriage, migration and gender* (pp. 180–212). New Delhi: Sage.

Ginn, J., Arber, S., Brannen, J., Dale, A., Dex, S., Elias, P., et al. (1996). Feminist fallacies: A reply to Hakim on women's employment. *British Journal of Sociology, 47*(1), 167–173.

Hakim, C. (1991). Grateful slaves and self made women: Fact and fantasy in women's work orientation. *European Sociological Review, 7*(2), 101–121.

Hakim, C. (1995). Five feminist myths about women's employment. *British Journal of Sociology, 46*(3), 429–455.

Hakim, C. (1996a). The sexual division of labor and women's heterogeneity. *British Journal of Sociology, 47*(1), 178–188.

Hakim, C. (1996b). *Key issues in women's work: Female heterogeneity and the polarization of women's employment*. London: Athlone.

Hossfield, K. (1998). 'Their logic against them': Contradictions in sex, race and class in silicon valley. In K. Ward (Ed.), *Women workers and global restructuring* (pp. 149–178). Ithaca: ILR press.

Kalpagam, U. (2008). 'American *Varan*' marriages among tamil brahmans: Preferences, strategies and outcomes. In R. Patriwala & P. Uberoi (Eds.), *Marriage, migration and gender* (pp. 98–122). New Delhi: Sage.

Kandiyoti, D. (1988). Bargaining with patriarchy. *Gender and Society, 2*(3), 274–291.

Kenny, M. (1978). *Woman X two: How to cope with a double life.* Hamlyn: Middlesex.

Khattak, S. G. (1995). Militarisation, masculinity and identity in Pakisthan: Effects on women. In N. Khan & A. Shehrbano (Eds.), *Unveiling the issue: Pakisthani women's perspectives on social, political and ideological issues* (pp. 52–64). Lahore: ASR Publications.

Kibria, N. (1990). Power, patriarchy, and gender conflict in the vietnamese immigrant community. *Gender and Society, 4*(1), 9–24.

Lamphere, L. (1987). *From working daughters to working mothers.* Ithaca, NY: Cornell University Press.

Lewis, I. M. (1971). *Ecstatic religion.* Baltimore: Penguin Books.

Lim, L. Y. C. (1988). *The electronics industry in south-east Asia: Confounding the critics.* Working Paper No. 552, School of Business Administration, University of Michigan, Ann Arbour.

Lim, L. Y. C. (1990). Women's work in export factories: The politics of a cause. In Irene Tinker (Ed.), *Persistent inequalities: Women and world development* (pp. 101–119). Oxford: Oxford University Press.

Lin, V. (1986). *Health, women's work and industrialization: Women workers in the semiconductor industry in Singapore and Malaysia.* Working Paper No. 130, Michigan State University.

Mand, K. (2008). Marriage and migration through the life course: Experiences of widowhood, separation and divorce amongst transnational Sikh women. In R. Patriwala & P. Uberoi (Eds.), *Marriage, migration and gender* (pp. 286–302). New Delhi: Sage.

Mies, M. (1980). *Indian women and patriarchy.* New Delhi: Concept Publishing House.

Mies, M. (1986). *Patriarchy and accumulation on a world scale.* London: Zed Press.

Mikyoung, K. (2003). South Korean workers' labour resistance in the era of export-oriented industrialization, 1970–1980. *Development and Society, 32*(1), 77–101.

Minturn, L. (1993). *Sita's daughters : Coming out of purdah.* New York: Oxford University Press.

Mookerjee, N. (2006). Muktir Gaan, the raped woman and migrant identities of the Bangladesh war. In N.C. Behera (Ed.) *Gender, conflict and migration* (pp. 72–96). New Delhi: Sage.

Munshi, S. (1998). Wife/mother/daughter-in-law: Multiple avatars of homemaker in 1990s Indian advertising. *Media, Culture and Society, 20*(4), 573–591.

Murphy-Lawless, J., Oakes, L., & Brady, C. (2004). *Understanding how sexually active women think about fertility, sex and motherhood.* Crisis pregnancy agency report no. 6, Dublin.

National Sample Survey Organization. (2011). *Employment and unemployment situation in India: 2009–2010.* New Delhi: Ministry of Statistics and Programme Implementation, Government of India.

O'Kane, M. (2006). Gender, borders and transversality: The emrging women's movement in the Burma-Thailand Borderlands. In N. C. Behera (Ed.), *Gender, conflict and migration* (pp. 227–254). New Delhi: Sage.

Ong, A. (1988). The production of possession: Spirits and the multinational corporation in Malaysia. *American Ethnologist, 15*(1), 28–42.

Patriwala, R., & Uberoi, P. (2008). Exploring the links: Gender issues in marriage and migration. In R. Patriwala & P. Uberoi (Eds.), *Marriage, migration and gender* (pp. 23–60). New Delhi: Sage.

Percot, M. (2006). Indian Nurses in the Gulf: From job opportunity to life strategy, In Anuja Agrawal (Ed.) *Migrant Women and Work* (pp. 155–176). New Delhi/Thousand Oaks/London: Sage Publication.

Pessar, P.R. (1984). The linkage between the household and workplace in the experience of Dominican women in the U.S. *International Migration Review, 18,* 1188–1212.

Proctor, I., & Padefield, M. (1998). *Young adult women, work and family: Living a contradiction.* London: Mansell.

Rajasingham, D. (2000). Ambivalent empowerment: The tragedy of tamil women. In R. Manachanda (Ed.), *Women, war and peace in South Asia: Beyond victimhood to agency* (pp. 12–130). New Delhi: Sage.

Rajasingham-Senanayake, D. (2006). Between tamil and muslim: Women mediating multiple identities in a new war. In N. C. Behera (Ed.), *Gender, conflict and migration* (pp. 175–204). New Delhi: Sage.

Riessman, C.K. (2000). Stigma and every day resistance practices: Childless women in South India, *Gender and Society, 14*(1), 111–135.

Roberts, K. (1993). Career trajectories and the mirage of increased social mobility. In I. Bates & G. Riseborough (Eds.), *Youth and inequality* (pp. 229–245). Buckimham: Open University Press.

Sabbah, F. (1984). *Women in the muslim unconscious, (trans) Mary Jo Lakeland.* New York: Pergamon Press.

Saigol, R. (2000). *At home or in the grave: Afghan women and the reproduction of patriarchy.* Paper presented at a WISCOMP Conference on 'Women and Security', New Delhi.

Seymour, S. (1999). *Women, family and child care in India: A world I transition.* Cambridge: Cambridge University Press.

Simon, H.A. (1955). A behavioural model of rational choice. *Quarterly Journal of Economics, 69(1),* 99–118.

Simon, H.A. (1956). Rational choice and the structure of the environment. *Psychological Review, 63*(2), 129–138.

Takhar, S. (2003). South Asian women and the question of political organization. In N. Puwar & P. Rahuram (Eds.), *South Asian women in the diaspora* (pp. 215–226). New York: Berg.

Thapan, M. (2005). 'Making incomplete': Identity, woman and the state. In M. Thapan (Ed.) *Transnational migration and politics of identity* (pp. 23–62). New Delhi: Sage Publications.

Thiruchnadran, S. (1999). State policy and the nature of female migration. In A. Chaudhury (Ed.), *On the margins: refugee, migrants and minorities.* Dhaka: RMMRU, Dhaka University.

Walby, S. (1997). *Gender transformations.* London: Routledge.

Ward, K.B. (1986). *Women and transnational corporation employment—A world system and feminist analysis.* Women in International Development Working Paper No. 120, Michigan State University.

Chapter 4
Nabadiganta: Women Workers in Kolkata's IT Sector

Abstract This chapter traces the growth and importance of the IT sector in India, and its development in Kolkata. It describes the socioeconomic characteristics of the women respondents surveyed, and discusses controversial issues such as gender relations at the workplace, gender differentials in wages, sexual harassment, work–household balance, childcare, leisure hours and the impact of outsourcing restrictions on the agency of women. The chapter discusses our survey findings to illuminate these issues, and repudiates the negative image of the IT sector created by the popular media.

Keywords Wage gap · Childcare · Work relations

4.1 Information Technology Industry in India

The IT sector is one of the most significant growth catalysts for the Indian economy. It is one of the major driving forces behind India's economic growth. In addition, this industry is also improving the lives of its employees by generating employment and increasing standard of living. The industry has played a significant role in transforming the Indian economy to a modern knowledge-based economy capable of supplying world-class technology and business services.

4.1.1 Role of Government Policy in Promoting IT Sector

Motivated by national security concerns, the industrial policy of the 1960s and 1970s tried to attain self-sufficiency in IT and electronics. An electronics committee was created to ensure that India could give up its dependence on advanced foreign products and technology and produce indigenous technology in a decade. Initially, the government tried to get IBM to share equity with local capital. When

Z. Husain and M. Dutta, *Women in Kolkata's IT Sector*,
SpringerBriefs in Sociology, DOI: 10.1007/978-81-322-1593-6_4,
© The Author(s) 2014

such attempts failed, companies like IBM and ICL started to refurbish old computers and sell or lease them. Indian customers preferred these cheap, refurbished computers to importing dearer, advanced computers—leading, ironically, to technological backwardness. In response, in the 1970s, the government established a Department of Electronics and a new electronics commission. One of its first step was setting up the Santa Cruz Electronics Export Processing Zone (SEEPZ). Investors in India were offered incentives to establish an export base there. Among other major steps were the establishment of the state-owned Electronics Corporation of India Ltd. (ECIL) and the use of the Foreign Exchange and Regulations Act (FERA) to challenge the monopoly of MNCs in the industry. Unfortunately, the latter led to the departure of IBM from India, which led to opening up the market to domestic competition. The decline of ECIL—partly due to its lack of cost-effectiveness and inefficiency—also forced the government to permit private firms to manufacture data processing systems and components.

Another important development was the export of software export services and products from the mid-1970s. Although import taxes raised the price of such exports and restricted it, India was the only developing country to export software services in the early 1980s, mainly because of low cost and proficiency in English.

4.1.2 Liberalisation and Growth of the IT Sector

The first wave of economic liberalisation led to the adoption of policies that viewed the IT industry as a core sector of the Indian economy. The removal of many restrictions to liberalise the Indian economy gave a substantial impetus to the IT sector. The relaxed policies made it easier for foreign capital to flow into this industry and for the considerable Indian diaspora to involve itself in it, stimulating its growth. To encourage growth of the IT industry, the government also offered incentives such as reduced import duties on software and hardware products. Software technology parks were established. Deregulation of the telecom sector was another major step. The government encouraged private investment in the creation of telecom infrastructure, while free market competition helped to drive down prices, improve subscriber experience and increase telephony penetration across the country.

As a result, India's IT industry picked up from the 1990s (NASSCOM 2010, 2012). In 1990–1991, the services of the industry were estimated at USD 150 million. Subsequent policy changes also helped to sustain its growth. Fiscal and procedural issues were relaxed further. In 2005, the Special Economic Zone (SEZ) Act was introduced—with special provisions for the BPO industry—and steps taken to ensure the availability of skilled labour to meet its manpower requirements. By 2006–2007, the industry has grown to USD 50 billion—a 330-fold increase in only 15 years. By 2008, the industry was estimated to increase to USD 87 billion (NASSCOM 2010, 2012).

Other factors have contributed to the growth of IT in India. India has the second largest technically qualified manpower with English-language skills (estimated at over 4 million). This provides incentives to firms in the US and other countries to set up and manage their units in India. The cost of labour is perhaps one-tenth of that in the US, and other business expenses are lower in India than in developed economies. India's internet bandwidth and costs are comparable with the best in the world. Many local governments participate in the growth of the IT industry and have set up IT parks that have the infrastructure that participating companies need for functioning smoothly.

Indian IT companies like Infosys Technologies, Wipro Technologies, TCS Ltd., CMC, HCL, etc. have demonstrated their competitiveness in the international market. India's own domestic IT sector is also witnessing rapid growth. Bangalore, Hyderabad and Chennai in the south have seen unimaginable growth in the IT sector.

4.2   Contribution of the IT Sector to the Indian Economy

The revenue earned by the IT industry from the domestic industry and from exports is given in Table 4.1.

The revenue earned by the IT sector as a percentage of GDP has increased from 1.2 % in 1998 to 7.5 % in 2012 (Table 4.2).

The IT sector also provides significant support to India's balance of payments position and is one of the major earners of foreign exchange. Exports from the IT sector comprised 25 % of India's exports in 2012, a substantial increase from 4 % in 1998. Revenue from IT exports constituted 17.8 % of current account receipts in 2008–2009 (Fig. 4.1). The increase in IT export earnings has relieved the pressure on private transfer receipts (the primary source of foreign exchange earnings for the Indian economy). The contribution of the IT sector is all the more important as it has helped to compensate for the decline in earnings from merchandise trade and other services.

The growth in exports and foreign investment has not only fuelled growth of the IT sector, but has also generated various types of externalities, along with multiplier effects. This has added to domestic production capabilities, growth of new firms in the country, new employment opportunities and creation of a brand image (Pazhayathodi 2012). Multiplier effects on hotel, tourism, transport, construction, banking and other sectors have fuelled overall growth of the Indian economy.

Further, being a labour-intensive sector, the IT industry has generated considerable employment opportunities. Employment in the IT sector has grown from 12 lakh in 2006 to 22 lakh in 2009 (Fig. 4.2). In addition, the sector generates more than 8.2 million jobs in support activities, such as transportation, security and catering (NASSCOM 2010).

There are other benefits. The 2012 NASSCOM (National Association of Software and Services Companies) Strategic Review observes:

Table 4.1 Revenue generated by IT sector from domestic and foreign markets

Financial year	IT services	BPO	Software products and engineering services	Hardware	Total
Domestic (Rs. Billion)					
2007	248	49	72	44	728
2008	317	63	90	414	884
2009	378	89	123	413	1003
2010	423	108	131	426	1088
2011	500	127	159	534	1320
2012	580	148	180	615	1523
Exports (USD billion)					
2007	17	8	7	0.5	32
2008	22	10	8	0.5	41
2009	26	12	10	0.4	47
2010	27	12	10	0.4	50
2011	22	10			50
2012	40	16	13	0.3	69

Source NASSCOM (2010, 2012)

Table 4.2 Revenue generated by IT sector (USD billion)

Financial year	Domestic	Exports	Percentage of GDP
2008	22	41	6.4
2009	22	47	6.7
2010	24	50	6.5
2011	29	50	7.1
2012	32	69	7.5

Source NASSCOM (2012)

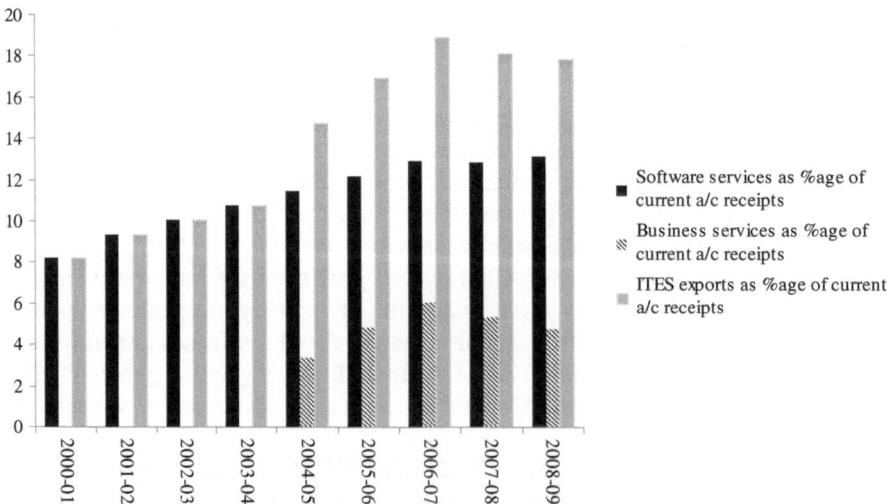

Fig. 4.1 India's ITES exports and current account services (*Source* Pazhayathodi (2012), p. 82)

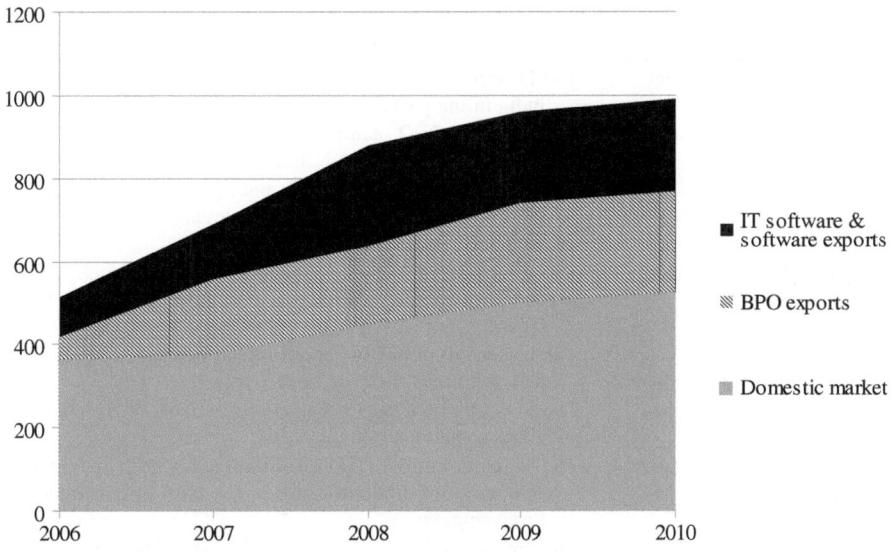

Fig. 4.2 Professionals employed in the IT sector (*Source* NASSCOM (2010))

In addition to fuelling India's economy, this industry is also positively influencing the lives of its people through an active direct and indirect contribution to the various socioeconomic parameters such as employment, standard of living and diversity among others. The industry has played a significant role in transforming India's image from a slow moving bureaucratic economy to a land of innovative entrepreneurs and a global player in providing world-class technology solutions and business services. The industry has helped India transform from a rural and agriculture-based economy to a knowledge-based economy (NASSCOM 2012).

The 2010 Strategic Review (NASSCOM 2010) summarises the multi-fold impact of the IT industry on the Indian economy (Table 4.3).

This discussion reveals that the IT sector has emerged as one of the core sectors of the Indian economy. Among its benefits is the rapid growth it generates in employment opportunities, which provides an opportunity to integrate women into the growth process. We will now see how far the concept of integrating women in development has worked for this sector.

4.3 A New Horizon?

According to a NASSCOM survey (NASSCOM 2003), only about 21 % of software professionals in software companies were women. This increased to 30 % of the total employee base in the IT industry in 2010 (NASSCOM 2010). The survey also indicated that the ratio of male to female workers in the ITES sector was 35:65 (NASSCOM 2003).

Table 4.3 Multi-fold impact of the IT sector on the Indian economy

Channel	Impact
Attract foreign investment	The IT sector accounted for over 10 % of the FDI received by India in the past decade
Develop source economies	The Indian IT-BPO sector helped clients in the US and Europe save over USD 25–30 billion in 2009
Increase R&D	The world's largest software corporations have established their business units in India, employing around 20 % of their total workforce in India
Contribute to local economy	The revenue from the IT sector for states with a large number of IT firms in 2009–2010 was more than 14 % of the state's GDP
Increase employment opportunities in rural areas	The number of rural BPO employees is expected to grow more than ten times over the next 3 years
Enable growth of technical education	The IT sector provides incentives to students of technical education courses
Contribute to growth of other sectors	The IT sector infused USD 2.7 billion during 2007–2009 in the economies of different states in the form of construction, furnishing, etc.
Develop infrastructure	The presence of the IT sector in select states has led to a tele-density level 50 % higher than the Indian average, and a broadband penetration level 100 % higher than in non-IT-intensive states
Increase exports	IT exports touched USD 50 billion, comprising almost 25 % of Indian exports
Strong tax contributions	The IT industry contributed USD 4.2 billion to the exchequer in 2009–2010 in the form of corporate tax payments and direct taxes paid by employees
Generate direct and indirect employment	The industry provides direct employment to more than 2.3 lakh persons in India. Indirect employment is more than 8 million persons

Source NASSCOM (2010)

An analysis of National Sample Survey Organization (NSSO) data by Basant and Rani (2004) reveals that the proportion of female workers in all categories was much lower than that of males. The share of women workers was particularly low among system analysts and programmers (Table 4.4). More detailed data show that the trends in the growth of women workers are also not very encouraging and reveal a clear gender divide. Growth of IT occupation workers during the 1990s was lower for women workers (17.5 %) than for male workers (26 %). Basant and Rani's analysis also reveals that the share of female workers in total workers in IT industry has declined from about 20–16 % (Basant and Rani 2004). Relative decline was most significant among professional workers, and there was a shift of female workers in clerical and related activities. Until 1999–2000, the impact of the high absorption of women workers in the ITES segment had quite likely not become evident and may be reflected in the 60th round data (Basant and Rani 2004, p. 5323).

Table 4.4 Distribution of IT workers by industrial/occupational categories and sex: 1999–2000

Classification system	Categories	Percentage			No. of workers ('000)
		Male	Female	Total	
Industrial categories	Hardware consultancy	70.6	29.4	100	15.8
	Software consultancy	88.1	11.9	100	124.2
	Data processing	82.2	17.8	100	56.9
	Database activities	86.4	13.6	100	28.5
	Maintenance and repair	86.1	13.9	100	21.4
	Other computer-related activities	68.7	31.3	100	18.7
	Total	84.1	15.9	100	265.7
Occupational categories	Stenographers, typists and card and tape punching operators	77.8	22.2	100	501.2
	Computing machine operators	77.5	22.5	100	293.8
	System analysts and programmers	93.2	6.8	100	75.5
	Total	79.1	20.9	100	870.6

Source Basant and Rani (2004), p. 5319

4.4 Nabadiganta: IT Sector in Kolkata

In the past decade, growth of the IT sector has also spread to other states in India. For instance, West Bengal has registered steady growth in the IT sector, concentrated in the metropolitan city of Kolkata, with a compound annual growth rate (CAGR) of 115 % in the 5 years between 1996 and 2001. It presently has a share of 3 % of total national exports. Most of the IT firms in Kolkata are located in Nabadiganta (New Dawn), in Salt Lake. The IT sector has grown in Kolkata for several reasons.

(1) **West Bengal possesses a sizeable talent pool of good quality**

West Bengal has a huge pool of quality talent and has historically enjoyed very low attrition rates.

(a) *Highest per capita spending on education* West Bengal has the highest per capita spending on education among large Indian states. This is reflected in the huge annual intake of undergraduate and postgraduate students. In 2009, there were 9,26,909 students enrolled in graduate courses, of which 56,001 were enrolled in courses in engineering, architecture, technology or design; at the postgraduate level, 6,939 out of 85,212 students were enrolled in these courses (GoI 2011).

(b) *Number of graduate colleges* In 2009, West Bengal had 841 degree colleges (of which 73 were engineering colleges) and 57 polytechnics (GoI 2011), with two of its educational institutes, Presidency University and St. Xavier's College, ranked among the top 10 degree colleges in India. In addition, premium educational institutes like the Indian Institute of Technology, Kharagpur (IIT-KGP), Indian Institute of Management, Calcutta (IIMC) and the Indian Statistical Institute (ISI) are located in the state.

(c) *Domain knowledge in financial services, travel/logistics* The local talent has domain knowledge in verticals such as financial services and travel/logistics.

As a result, the talent available in this region is of high quality: over 20 % of students at the Indian Institutes of Technology (IIT) and a significant section of the Non-Resident Indian (NRI) entrepreneurship at Silicon Valley belongs to this region.

(2) **Operating in Kolkata is cheaper than in other metropolitan cities**

Kolkata offers ITES players one of the lowest operation costs in the country. This is reflected in the low Centre for Monitoring Indian Economy (CMIE) consumer price indices, compared to other key ITES destinations in the country (355 for Kolkata compared to 454 for Chennai, 413 for Bangalore, 410 for Hyderabad and 401 for Delhi).

Salaries for fresh graduates in Kolkata are about 10–15 % lower than in other metros. Also, the low attrition levels in Kolkata (10 % as compared to industry benchmarks of about 20 % in the IT industry) work in its favour by reducing the training costs incurred by employers.

(3) **West Bengal has high quality infrastructure**

Kolkata offers about 580 Mbps of international satellite connectivity through Videsh Sanchar Nigam Limited (VSNL) and Software Technology Park of India (STPI). About 70 % of this bandwidth is available to new players. Cable connectivity is provided through leased Bharat Sanchar Nigam Limited (BSNL) lines of 92 Mbps to Mumbai and onward connectivity through submarine cables landing at Mumbai. Besides BSNL, private players like Reliance Infocom and Bharti Telesonic plan to connect Kolkata through their own National Long Distance (NLD) backbone to Chennai and Mumbai. Additional cable connectivity will also be provided by Railtel, which will provide bandwidth to the telecom carriers. In addition, highly reliable local loop options are available from BSNL, STPI WLL/ OFC.[1]

Data on the employment of women in Kolkata—or even the state—is not available, but we may safely assume that the growth of the IT sector in the city has provided employment to many women. In this study, we examine the impact of employment in the IT sector on the empowerment of women. The next section describes the profile of our respondents. This is followed by an analysis of the responses.

---

[1] Based on http://www.indianchamber.org/northeast/ITWestBengal.pdf accessed on 20 October 2012.

4.5 Profile of Women Workers Surveyed in Kolkata's IT Sector

We found that all the respondents had urban backgrounds. About 69 % resided in Kolkata, while 9 % came from the suburbs. Other towns in West Bengal provided 9 % of respondents, while 13 % of the sample had been transferred from outside the state.

In line with earlier studies of the IT sector, we found that the workforce is quite young. The mean and median ages are 27 and 26 years, respectively. This is same for all segments. Only among the call centres is the age slightly lower—both mean and median are 24 years. Given that the boom in Calcutta's IT sector is a recent phenomenon, this is expected.

Although variations in the age of respondents are not marked, differences in length of work experience are observed across segments (Table 4.5). This implies that the age of entry in both the IT sector and company vary across different IT sectors. Specifically, the age of joining the IT sector and the present company is lowest for call centre employees. This is not surprising given that educational qualifications required for joining call centres is very low, thereby permitting entry at a young age.

About 40 % of the respondents are married. This proportion is relatively high in the software sector (65 %) but low in the miscellaneous category (14 %) and call centre category (6 %). The average family size is about four, for both married and unmarried respondents. About 36 % of ever-married respondents (that is, currently married or divorced) had one child, while 6 % had two children. Predictably, employees in the software development and KPO sectors were found to have children. This does not indicate that employees of call centres and in the miscellaneous sector have lower fertility. What is more likely is that such individuals generally marry and have children *after leaving* these sectors.

We next turn to the educational profile of the respondents. This has an important influence on their agency and empowerment. Although the demand for more companionate wives in nineteenth century India led to women's education (Mies 1980; Mukhopadhyay and Seymour 1994), the outcome of such education had complex and unintended consequences. Education generally (though not necessarily) raises the age of first marriage so that the bride is a mature woman capable of forming her own opinions and exercising independent judgement, who may challenge the authority of her husband, in-laws and (even) their parents (Mukhopadhyay and Seymour 1994). Ulrich (1994), for instance, documents the case of Havik Brahmin women: on gaining education, these women started challenging the institution of arranged marriage, demanded the right to work outside the village and expressed their preference for nuclear families after marriage.

The majority of respondents (68 %) were educated in English-medium schools and were proficient in English. Predictably, the proportion of respondents with English-medium education is relatively high in the KPO sector (84 %) and in the

Table 4.5 Age and experience of respondents (in years)

Company code		Age	Tenure in IT sector	Age of joining IT sector	Tenure in company	Age of joining company
Software	Mean	27	4	24	3	25
development	Median	27	4	23	2	25
KPO[a]	Mean	27	5	23	2	26
	Median	27	3	25	1	26
BPO[b]	Mean	27	3	24	2	25
	Median	26	2	24	1	25
Call centre	Mean	24	2	22	1	23
	Median	24	1	23	1	23
Misc	Mean	29	3	26	2	27
	Median	27	3	25	1	26
Total	Mean	**27**	**3**	**23**	**2**	**25**
	Median	**26**	**3**	**24**	**1**	**25**

[a] Knowledge Process Outsourcing (KPO) is a form of outsourcing in which knowledge—or information-related work is carried out by workers in a different company in the same country or at an off-shore location to save cost. This typically involves high-value work carried out by highly skilled staff

[b] Business Process Outsourcing refers to the transmission of processes along with the associated operational activities and responsibilities to a third party with a guaranteed level of service

call centre sector (77 %) because the ability to speak English is an essential qualification in these sectors. The proportion of respondents educated in English-medium school is relatively low in the BPO sector (50 %).

There are sharp variations in educational profile across the five segments studied (Table 4.6). In software, essentially a technical profession, 84 % of respondents are technical graduates or postgraduates. In the KPO sector, 76 % are graduates or better educated. Interestingly, the proportion of postgraduates is low in both these segments—22 % in software companies and 24 % in KPOs. Quite a high proportion of KPO employees (52 %) have also completed postgraduation. About three out of every four BPO employees interviewed is a graduate. Call centre employees comprise a heterogeneous category in terms of their educational attainment. They may be divided into three almost equal categories—high school graduates, graduates and postgraduates.

In addition, about 22 % of the respondents have acquired management diplomas or certificates. This proportion is relatively high among KPO employees—about 44 have some sort of management education. During our survey we observed that the English education and (in case of software engineers) technical education imparted a sense of confidence and self-belief in the respondents. This led the more educated respondents to evaluate options (including challenges to patriarchy) maturely and act in accordance with such evaluation. On the other hand, the 'smart' culture of call centres made their employees independent and assertive.

We also found the economic status of respondents to be high. About 70 % live in their own houses, while 29 % of the respondents own a car. Six respondents had

Table 4.6 Educational level of respondents

Educational level	Software development	KPO	BPO	Call centre	Misc	Total
High school graduates	2.7	4	3.6	29.4	14.3	7.9
Graduate	2.7	24	75	23.5	42.9	30.7
Technical graduate	62.2	8	–	–	–	21.9
Management graduate	2.7	8	–	5.9	–	3.5
Postgraduate (PG)	8.1	52	17.9	35.3	42.9	26.3
Technical PG	21.6	–	–	–	–	7
Technical Diploma/Certificate	–	4	3.6	5.9	–	2.6

vacationed abroad in the year preceding the survey, while two-thirds had gone for a vacation outside West Bengal (or home state, in case of migrants). While the respondents from the software segment were most well off (73 % owned a house, and 51 % owned a car), respondents from the miscellaneous category appeared least well off (only 43 % owned a house, while 14 % owned a car). Not surprisingly, 57 % of the respondents from this sector are dissatisfied with their living standards, as compared to 42 % for the entire sample. In general, satisfaction with the level of living standards is high among employees in the KPO sector and in call centres (72 and 71 %, respectively).

Our results, therefore, corroborate the findings of earlier studies that women workers in the IT sector belong to an exclusive socio-economic class. Studies undertaken by Krishna and Brihmadesam (2006) and Upadhya (2007) observes that the majority of respondents hail from high caste, educated and affluent urban families. As a respondent admitted,

> I have very rarely seen women coming from a rural background … at most they come from suburbs. Women do not come from a typical rural background … father teaching in primary school, mother has not studied. Women in the IT sector come from the urban middle class.

Respondents opined that the possible reason for this bias is that investment in girls' higher education and coaching for is considered a luxury in low-income and rural households, and that such families are often averse to the idea of their daughters availing hostel-based education. The nature of the recruitment process was another contributory factor. The reliance on campus interviews and the importance placed on communication skill and the ability to communicate in English during the recruitment process limits the socioeconomic base from which women workers are recruited.

The background of the women workers—in particular their economic status, urban background and educational attainment—is very important in determining the nature of their aspirations and how they interact with their social and working environment to create a structured individuation (Roberts 1993).

4.6 Working in the IT Sector

Most respondents were attracted to the IT sector by its prospects (24 %) and high pay (20 %). Consistency with educational profile was another important reason, particularly among software engineers, along with the challenge that working in the IT sector posed. But how far did the working environment satisfy the respondents? This question may be examined from different angles.

4.6.1 Discrimination in Earnings

The literature reviewed in Chap. 2 argues that discrimination in earnings is a major form of exploitation of women workers in export-based industries. A natural starting point to our analysis of the conditions of women workers in the IT sector is to examine whether such wage-based discrimination exists in that sector.

Our questionnaire did not have a question on the amount of earnings because (1) attempts to collect information on earnings through surveys are generally not very successful and may even alienate respondents and (2) the companies that had permitted us to interview their employees and the officers who facilitated such interaction, too, had requested us not to seek information on pay structures. However, it posed the statement 'There is salary differential across gender' and asked respondents if they agreed with it. We found that only one out of ten respondents agreed with this statement, while the majority (84 %) disagreed with it. Thus, women workers do not perceive any discrimination regarding salary. In general, the majority of respondents (74 %) felt that gender was not considered while determining the reward or compensation package. Although this is not surprising, given the formal nature of job contracts, we tried to cross-check this response using secondary data.

As mentioned in Chap. 1, NSSO surveys on 'Employment and unemployment' provide reliable data on education, occupation and earnings of workers. We used this data to examine whether there are gender differences in earnings in the IT sector.

The NSSO collects data on weekly earnings. Dividing weekly earnings by seven, we get the daily earnings of workers in the IT sector. Surprisingly, the mean wage of women workers (Rs. 2,444) is higher than that of men workers (Rs. 1,853) in 2004–2005. In the case of sample estimates, it is not enough to compare figures— we also have to test whether the difference can be generalised to the population as a whole using statistical means. The standard t-test is one way of testing whether differences in sample means reflects differences in population means. The observed difference is statistically significant at 1 % level (as the absolute value of the t-statistic, 1.6747, is lower than the tabulated value of t at 5 % level). In 2009–2010, in contrast, we find that men workers earn more than women workers (Rs. 2,114, against Rs. 1,587). But when we test whether the difference is statistically signif-icant, we find that the t-statistic is only 0.9821. Since this is below the tabulated value at 10 % level, the difference is *not* statistically significant.

One limitation of this method of analysis and statistical testing is that it does not consider that differences in earnings may also reflect differences in experience and education of respondents. This limitation can be remedied by adopting multivariate methods—specifically by estimating a regression model of daily earnings on gender, education and experience of respondent using the Ordinary Least Squares (OLS) method. Normally, we use log of earnings—rather than earnings— as the dependent variable. The logic is to minimise the extent of variations in earnings and obtain more precise results.

Another issue in estimating the regression model is that the NSSO does not solicit information on experience. To solve this problem, we take age as a proxy for experience. Obviously, the extent to which this solution is valid will depend upon the extent to which respondents change occupations (move from one sector to another). Although empirical studies have observed a high attrition rate within the Indian IT sector, such movements generally occur within the sector between one IT company to another, and not from the IT sector to outside the sector (or the reverse). We have also taken square of AGE to test whether wage increase slows down, or accelerates, with experience.

Thus, the regression model estimated takes the form:

$$\text{LEARNING} = \alpha + \beta_1 \text{FEMALE} + \beta_2 \text{AGE} + \beta_3 \text{AGE2} + \beta_4 \text{HIGH SCHOOL}$$
$$+ \beta_5 \text{DIPLOMA} + \beta_6 \text{GRADUATE} + \beta_7 \text{PG}$$

$$(4.1)$$

when:

LEARNING	log of daily earnings
FEMALE	dummy for gender of respondent, $= 1$ for Females, $= 0$ for Males
AGE	Age of respondent
HIGH SCHOOL	(dummy) $= 1$ if respondent has passed Higher Secondary level (corresponding to 12 years of education) and $= 0$ otherwise
DIPLOMA	(dummy) $= 1$ if respondent has acquired any Diploma and $= 0$ otherwise
GRADUATE	(dummy): $= 1$ if respondent is a graduate, and $= 0$ otherwise
PG (dummy)	$= 1$ if respondent is a postgraduate, or has higher education, and $= 0$ otherwise

The coefficient of FEMALE indicates whether women workers are paid lower wages than their male counterparts. If the coefficient of FEMALE (β_1) is negative, then women workers get lower wages, while a positive value of β_1 indicates that it is women who are being paid a higher wage. However, can we generalise? In other words, we need to test whether the value of the coefficient would have been positive or negative had we used data on all workers in the IT sector instead of using a sample—by considering the value of the t-ratio and checking if the corresponding probability value is less than 0.10. If this condition is satisfied, we can

Table 4.7 Results of regression model of log daily earnings on education, gender and education: 2004–2005 and 2009–2010

Variable	61st round			66th round		
	Coefficient	t	Prob.	Coefficient	t	Prob.
FEMALE	0.17	1.38	0.17	−0.28	−1.61	0.11
AGE	0.21	4.16	0.00	0.10	1.78	0.08
AGE^2	0.00	−3.59	0.00	0.00	−1.52	0.13
BELOW HIGH SCHOOL (Ref. Cat.)						
HIGH SCHOOL	0.58	2.65	0.01	−0.01	−0.03	0.98
DIPLOMA	0.68	3.43	0.00	−0.01	−0.04	0.97
GRADUATE	1.29	7.84	0.00	0.45	2.43	0.02
POSTGRADUATE	1.34	6.93	0.00	0.69	2.78	0.01
INTERCEPT	2.59	3.09	0.00	5.50	5.99	0.00
N	264			144		
F	17.09		0.00	4.24		0.00
R^2	0.32			0.18		

generalise our observations to the IT sector. On the other hand, if the probability value is greater than 0.10, our results hold only for the NSSO sample and should not be generalised to the IT sector as a whole. The regression model (4.1) is estimated for each round separately (Table 4.7).

Results reveal that wage increases with experience (proxied by age), but the increase is not linear. Rather, the wage increase decelerates with age. In the 61st round, wages also increase with educational level. However, in the 66th round, only respondents with graduate level or higher levels of education are paid more than diploma holders or those with at most 12 years of education.

The variable of interest to us is FEMALE. In the 61st round, its value is positive, implying that women are paid higher wages than men. In the 66th round, on the other hand, the coefficient is negative, implying that women are paid less than men in the post-recession period. This is consistent with the results obtained earlier. However, and this is crucial, *in none of the two models are these differences statistically significant.* This implies that the observed difference in wages across gender holds only for the sample, and not for the population. In other words, analysis of NSSO data corroborates the perception of our respondents that there is no discrimination in earnings.

4.6.2 Career Development

Employees consider career growth prospects important along with the financial package of the job. We asked respondents whether they felt that their career development was consistent with their educational profile—28 % felt their career growth matched their educational profile perfectly, while a further 34 % were satisfied with their career growth. However, a fifth of respondents were unhappy with their career growth. About 17 % of the respondents refused to comment.

In Chap. 3, we saw that researchers are concerned over a glass ceiling in the IT sector that restricts the career growth of women workers after a point. In our survey, when we specifically asked about career plateauing[2] and the glass ceiling, the response was ambiguous. About two-fifths did not agree there was career plateauing, while 35 % agreed that this is a major issue; 24 % were uncertain. The main reasons cited for career plateauing were the inability to cope with the twin pressures of balancing work and household responsibilities, followed by gender discrimination and inability to move outside state. When asked whether women had to work harder (than men), however, 54 % of the respondents disagreed, while 40 % agreed with the statement. The response to the query whether career advancement was more difficult for women was also ambiguous—49 % disagreed and 40 % agreed. Women's inability to work the long hours of the IT industry has often been cited as an important reason for their stunted career development. About 46 % of our respondents agreed that the long working hours posed a problem for women workers, while half the respondents disagreed.

Mobility of the employee, particularly the ability to join companies outside the home state, is another major prerequisite for moving up the ladder. We found that although 64 % of the respondents had been offered a job outside their home state, only 29 % of respondents who received such offers accepted those. Further, some of these respondents were 'following' their husbands, who had either been transferred outside their home state or had accepted a job there. Most respondents said they declined such offers for family reasons.

The attitude of women workers towards female team leaders is also somewhat ambiguous. About 23 % are not comfortable with working under female team leaders, while 33 % do not have any such objections. A large proportion of respondents (41 %) are undecided.

When asked about obstacles to their career, household responsibilities were cited in 50 % cases. Such responsibilities included the need to look after children or elderly parents, for spending time with husbands or for social interaction. Interestingly, a third of such respondents emphasised the lack of social life, rather than looking after parents or children or spending time with husbands. Only 11 % of respondents mentioned security and late hours each as hindrances to their career growth.

Despite such problems, more than 40 % of the respondents want to remain in the IT sector until their retirement. The majority of the respondents who wanted to leave the sector are call centre employees. In this group, we found 59 % of respondents wanted to leave the sector. Common factors motivating the desire to leave the IT sector are monotony of the work (particularly among BPO employees), work pressure (among KPO employees), career plateauing (cited by

---

[2] Career plateauing refers to the flattening off of the career growth curve for women after a point, primarily due to pregnancy and childrearing.

employees in the miscellaneous group) and health-related problems (among call centre employees).

Attrition rates, however, are quite high. On an average, respondents have changed jobs at least once. This works to about 1.5 years in each company. Attrition rates are relatively higher among employees of the KPO and miscellaneous sectors. On an average, respondents have changed jobs twice in these two sectors. This works out to an average tenure of 1 year in each company for employees in the miscellaneous sector. Average tenure in the KPO sector, however, is about the same as in other IT sectors (Table 4.2). Financial reasons and better career prospects are the main reasons for shifting jobs. This is uniformly true for all sectors. Organisational problems are also an important reason for changing jobs among call centre employees. Respondents were also asked whether they felt that high attrition rates among women reflected an inability to cope up with the work pressure. Half the respondents disagreed with this statement; only 34 % of respondents felt that this statement was true.

4.6.3 Working Environment

In Chap. 2, we saw that the gender division of work in the export-based industry was the mean through which women workers were exploited. In the IT sector, however, work allocation is reportedly not gender-specific—as most respondents (61 %) reported. But when the project involves relocating a worker, the management generally considers the difficulty that women may have for social and family reasons to relocate even for short periods. Work allocation becomes gender-specific if it involves relocation, 57 % of the respondents reported. Generally, married women and women with children are not sent on off-shore or other forms of on-site assignments. Unfortunately, this is often taken into consideration during career ratings, adversely affecting career development of such women. Respondents also reported that single women, and particularly married women whose children have grown up, accept such assignments.

In general, colleagues are reported to be supportive and cooperative (89 %), with only 15 % of respondents reporting that some male members of their team or office were offensive. Nevertheless, 28 % of respondents perceived their male colleagues to be condescending or patronising, with about 17 % being undecided; and 42 % of the respondents felt that male colleagues were sceptical about the efficiency of women workers.

4.6.4 Sexual Harassment

About 27 % of the respondents worked in jobs with changing shifts. This proportion was comparatively high among call centre (53 %) and KPO (40 %)

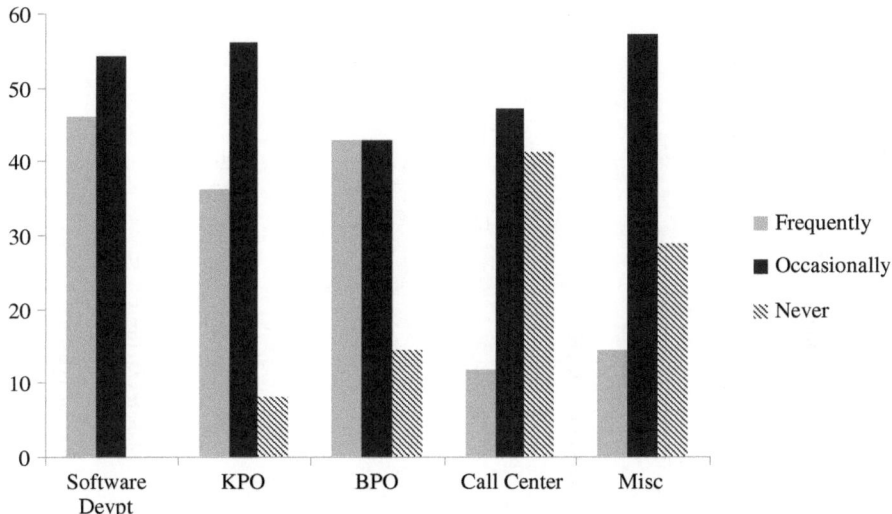

Fig. 4.3 Percentage of respondents working over-time—by sectors

employees. It was reported that 87 % had to work over-time—with 36 % working over-time frequently (Fig. 4.3). This proportion is particularly high among software engineers and BPO employees. In contrast, 47 and 57 % of employees in call centres and in the miscellaneous sector reported that they had to work extra time occasionally.

About a fifth of the respondents had to work night shifts—often referred to as the graveyard shift—and most were transported home. Most companies have a rule that women workers are not to be dropped off last. By and large this is followed. About 75 % of respondents were dropped off before the last male colleague. In several cases, the women workers themselves refused the offer as they felt that it would be imposing too much on their equally weary male colleagues—who may have to travel in a different direction. We were also informed that some workers, particularly single call centre and BPO employees, wanted to be dropped off near nightclubs or even on the Eastern Metropolitan Bypass, a lonely and dark stretch of road, where they had fixed a rendezvous with their boyfriend.

Travelling at night carries the risk of being harassed by the driver or other colleagues. Incidents of harassment by a male colleague were more common than harassment by drivers—25 respondents reported being harassed by colleagues, compared to five cases of harassment by the driver. There may be two reasons for this. First, drivers will not attempt to harass women in the presence of their male colleagues. The practice of dropping women workers last acts as effective protection from sexual harassment by the driver. Second, a driver can be traced easily; further, as he is not a valued member of the firm, companies are not reluctant to punish drivers. Five of our respondents had reported the driver for misbehaviour; the company took action in four cases. In contrast, action was taken on only half

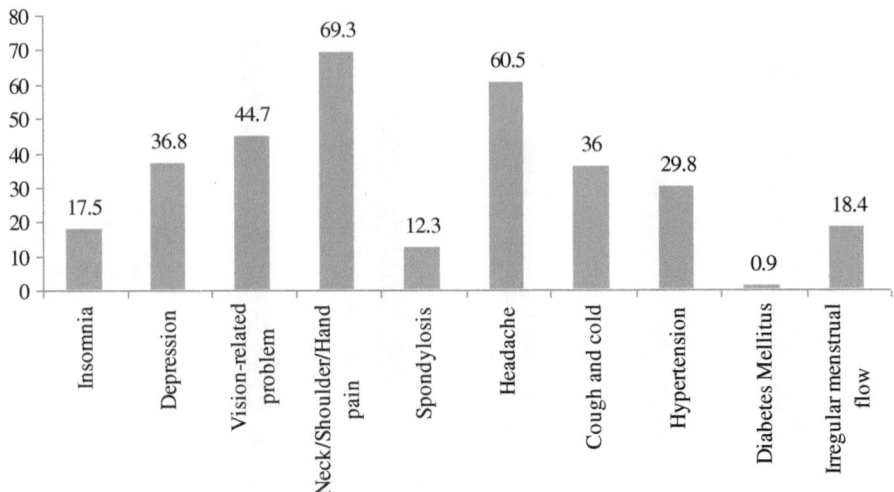

Fig. 4.4 Percentage of respondents suffering from different health ailments

the 10 complaints made against colleagues. Respondents reported that the company was reluctant to take action against colleagues with a good work record. In such cases, generally, the woman making the complaint was transferred to some other section or team.

The ineffectiveness of complaints (along with the desire to avoid scandal and gossip) is one reason why most harassment incidents go unreported. We found that 50 % of incidents involving drivers and 75 % of harassment by colleagues are not reported. Sexual harassment at the workplace is less frequent; only six cases were reported by respondents.

4.6.5 Health Problems

The prevalence of occupational disease reflects working conditions and the strains imposed on the worker. It is also an important indication of well-being. We observed that a high proportion of respondents suffered from depression (37 %), vision-related ailments (45 %), neck/shoulder pain (69 %), headache (61 %), cold (36 %) and hypertension (30 %) (Fig. 4.4). We should interpret these results carefully as they affect both genders and may not be unique to the IT sector but pertain to any desk job in an air-conditioned environment.

Before arriving at a firm conclusion about the epidemiological profile of women workers in the IT sector, we should also include male workers in the IT sector and women workers in other sectors as a control group. Although the focus on empowerment of women workers in the IT sector justifies this omission to some extent, the failure to include male workers in our sample remains a limitation of this study.

4.7 After Working Hours

The double shift, or twin pressures of shouldering both work and domestic responsibilities, has been a major issue with feminist researchers. It has been argued that women's participation in economic activities has reduced their leisure time.

The analysis of responses, however, does not bear this out. Only one of five women cooked regularly, 24 % did the laundry regularly and 18 % cleaned regularly. Such chores were generally undertaken occasionally (37, 26 and 25 %, respectively) or on holidays (25, 30 and 38 %, respectively). In fact, a fairly large proportion did not undertake these activities at all—14 % never cooked, 19 % never washed clothes and 18 % never dusted.

However, women workers did spend a great deal of time with their children. Of the 16 respondents with children, as many as 13 provided their children care services regularly, while the remaining three spent time with their children during holidays. Similarly, 64 % of women workers provided care services to elderly parents even on working days, while 34 % of respondents spent time with their parents occasionally or on holidays.

We sought information on the activities respondents undertook on holidays. The two most popular off-day activities are visiting shopping malls (21 %) and watching films (22 %). The entire family, including children and even elders (in-laws or parents), may undertake these activities. In contrast, socialising with relatives or friends and performing household chores (16 % in both cases) are activities less commonly undertaken.

Almost all respondents (94 %) feel that the long working hours and over-time affect their family life. In some cases, they even had to discontinue working briefly. About a fifth of respondents had not worked continually throughout their working career. This is a very high proportion given that the average tenure of working in the IT sector is about 3 years. The main reasons for the discontinuation are health related, family-related and marriage.

We asked respondents whether they felt that women were able to balance their work and household responsibilities; 79 % felt that they were, despite considerable difficulty. Respondents felt the biggest obstacle to attaining such balance was the lack of empathy and cooperation from superior officers and male colleagues—not from the family.

Within the household, women enjoy considerable autonomy. About 48 % of respondents decided how to spend their income, while a further 45 % undertook such decisions jointly. Only 7 % did not have any control over their earnings. Overall, 79 % of respondents were satisfied with their control in household decision-making. This is a very high figure.

4.8 Impact of Global Recession and Restrictions on Outsourcing

In 2009, the Obama administration announced a series of steps to reduce the soaring unemployment levels in the US. Among such steps were curbs on outsourcing. For instance, US companies hiring foreigners on temporary work permits (H-1B visas) will not be eligible to receive the benefits of the stimulus plan announced by Obama—the Administration will eliminate 'incentives for companies that ship jobs overseas'.

Such measures, along with the global recession, led to fears that the growth of the IT sector would be affected. The consequent slowdown in the industry would reduce employment prospects. Gender researchers warned that this might lead to discrimination between male and female workers at the entry point or in selecting workers for lay-offs. The consequent vulnerability, they felt, would have an adverse impact on the agency of women workers.[3]

It is true that recruitment in the IT industry has slowed down considerably. Moreover, the joining date for those selected by major IT companies is often postponed. However, discussion with IT sector workers failed to show that there is any gender discrimination in selection or such postponement. Nor has there been any lay-off based on gender. The US policies may have reduced work, but this was partly compensated by a shift to other markets. As a result, the fears of gender researchers have been proven unfounded.

4.9 Summing Up

To sum up, the main findings from the analysis of responses to the questionnaire-based interviews are as follows:

(a) Women working in the IT sector come from affluent urban households. Their average education level is graduation or above, and most of them have studied in English-medium schools. This indicates that such women are not typical of Indian—or even Bengali—society; rather they belong to an exclusive class.
(b) High pay and bright prospects led these women to join the IT sector.
(c) While these women face subtle forms of gender discrimination, male colleagues are generally supportive—though often condescending and sceptical of their ability.
(d) There is no discrimination with respect to pay or incentive structure or assignments. However, once again, there is a subtle bias against women. Gender is considered when allocating off-shore assignments and affects career growth. Family-related restrictions on inter-state mobility also hinder their upward mobility within the organisation.

---

[3] For instance, Jeemol Unni, in a comment on a presentation of an early draft of this work in the Annual Conference of the Indian Labour Economics Association in 2008.

(e) There is no evidence of a double shift in our findings. Few women workers perform household chores regularly. However, they take care of parents (or in-laws) and children and spend time with them; this is a regular activity that cuts into their leisure time. A large part of after-office hours are spent on activities like visiting shopping malls and watching movies.

(f) Women reported that they enjoy considerable autonomy within their families.

(g) Women acknowledge that work often conflicts with their household responsibilities. There does not seem to be any evidence to suggest that their husband or other family members create obstacles to their professional career. Rather, women would prefer more support from superior officers and colleagues. Overall, however, respondents claimed that they were able to balance work and home.

(h) Only respondents from the call centres are determined to quit the IT sector. Other respondents have a high attrition rate (mainly motivated by pay and prospects), but do not want to quit the sector in general.

Thus, the grim picture painted in Chap. 2—women working away as slaves in double shifts and being constantly exploited by both employers and relatives in an environment that is the synergistic creation of capitalism, globalisation and patriarchy—does not seem to hold for Kolkata. Nabadiganta does seem to be a new horizon—not a false dawn—with women being quite content with their career development, happy to remain in the IT sector and being able to balance work and home. But whether employment in the IT sector allows women workers to attain their aspirations and exercise their agency unfettered, or whether women satisfice—by adapting their aspirations and exercising their agency bearing their structural realities in mind—is examined in the next chapter.

References

Basant, R., & Rani, U. (2004). Labor market deepening in India's it: An exploratory analysis. *Economic and Political Weekly, XXXIX*(50), 5317–5326.

Government of India. (2011). *Statistics of higher and technical education: 2009–2010.* New Delhi: Ministry of Human Resources Development.

Krishna, A., & Brihmadesam, V. (2006). What does it take to be a software professional? *Economic and Political Weekly*, 19 July, 3307–3314.

Mies, M. (1980). *Indian women and patriarchy.* New Delhi: Concept Publishing House.

Mukhopadhyay, C. C., & Seymour, S. (1994). Introduction and theoretical overview. In C. C. Mukhopadhyay & S. Seymour (Eds.), *Women, education and family structure in India* (pp. 1–33). Boulder: Westview Press.

NASSCOM. (2003). *The IT-BPO sector in India: Strategic review.* New Delhi: NASSCOM.

NASSCOM. (2010). *The IT-BPO sector in India: Strategic review.* New Delhi: NASSCOM.

NASSCOM. (2012). *The IT-BPO sector in India: Strategic review.* New Delhi: NASSCOM.

Pazhayathodi, B. (2012). *Exports of services and off-shore outsourcing: An empirical investigation in the Indian context.* Occasional paper no. 156, Export Import Bank of India, Mumbai.

Roberts, K. (1993). Career trajectories and the mirage of increased social mobility. In Bates, I. & Riseborough, G. (Ed.) *Youth and Inequality* (pp. 229–245). Buckimham: Open University Press.

Ulrich, H. (1994). Asset and liability: The role of female education in changing marriage patterns among Havik Brahmins. In C. C. Mukhopadhyay & S. Seymour (Eds.), *Women, education and family structure in India* (pp. 187–212). Boulder: Westview Press.

Upadhya, C. (2007). Employment, exclusion and 'Merit' in the Indian IT industry. *Economic and Political Weekly*, 19 May, 1863–1868.

Chapter 5
Agency and Satisficing in Kolkata's IT Sector

Abstract This chapter applies the 'satisficing' framework (described in Chap. 3) to women workers in Kolkata's IT sector. It examines the economic and socio-cultural changes shaping the constraints that define which outcomes are satisfactory, and analyses the behavioural patterns of respondents to show—by analysing responses to questionnaire-based interviews and case studies—how women workers successfully balance multiple, conflicting activities and objectives. Their testimony reveals their agency on different fronts; we argue that this agency indicates progress in gender relations.

Keywords Agency · Behavioural patterns · Balancing work · Household

5.1 Satisficing in Kolkata's IT Sector

In the previous chapter we had argued that the women workers in Kolkata's IT sector satisfice. How they do so is examined in this chapter. We first examine the economic and cultural changes shaping the constraints defining which outcomes are satisfactory. This is followed by an analysis of the outcome(s) chosen.

5.1.1 Historical Background

If we look at the status of women in West Bengal from a historical angle, then we will see that the Bengal Renaissance initiated a change in their social position. The attempts of the social reformers and educationists to educate middle class Bengali women were not to ensure their autonomy and independence (Mies 1986) but to develop and educate a new breed of women who would be fit companions for their husbands and better mothers to their children (Basu and Amin 2000). Women of the nineteenth and early twentieth century were emancipated, but allowed carefully

monitored entry only in the social and cultural spheres. Any violations of the
carefully defined boundaries—as, for instance, Kadambini Ganguly's unaccompa-
nied visit to Edinburg to study medicine—was frowned upon by even social
reformers. The participation of women in economic activities was delayed to the
post-Second World War period. In the 1950s, economic pressures—in the form of
inflationary pressures and the economic distress amongst refugee families following
the partition of Bengal—forced opened the doors of the labour market to women.

Such women started working in fixed hour occupations like office clerks and
school teachers. Such work, however, did not preclude women from providing care
services at home. The persistence of the social norm may be attributed to the low
quality of employment and the fixed hours of work. The low pressure of work in
such occupations also permitted some degree of flexibility in working hours. The
absence of any social questioning of this dual role was another contributory factor.
These factors trivialised the conflict between the role of housewife and worker,
and ensured that women would continue to perform to undertake household
chores—albeit at the cost of sacrificing leisure hours.

5.1.2 Cultural Change and the Moulding of Expectations

Cultural forces facilitated the change in social attitudes towards women's education and employment. Starting from the 1980s the role of women was subject to a
critical review in the literature and in the popular media. On one hand, writers like
Tilottoma Majumdar, Suchitra Bhattacharya, Sangeeta Bandopadhyay and Bani
Basu established women as individual self-supporting characters independent of
males, with their own aspirations, desire and sexuality, and the means to achieve
them. Simultaneously, the films of Aparna Sen and Rituparno Ghosh examined
conformism and emancipation, as well as tabooed issues like female sexuality. The
new wave of feminist novels and films presented a definite and positive image of
the modern woman—professional and successful, confident and liberated, as
opposed to the passive stereotypes of patriarchy (Bhattacharya 2005). This questioning also found its way into television soap operas and women's magazines
(like *Sanonda*, *Paroma*, etc.) and started permeating the public consciousness. It
was only a matter of time that such cultural sanction would encourage women to
start questioning the repression of their identities and the imposition of the role of
care provider by a patriarchal society.

Four factors facilitated this step towards emancipation—particularly among
women from middle income families. First, as seen in Chap. 4, the respondents
surveyed hail from similar socio-economic and cultural background; this generates
similar aspirations about work and the family. Marriage, too, occurs to men from
similar class/sociocultural groups. The homogeneity in paternal and matrimonial
families reduces the possibility of conflict between norms. Moreover, attitude
towards women's education and employment too is similar between paternal and
matrimonial families.

The other factors facilitating the shift in attitude towards women and their individuality are as follows: (a) the shift in motives for working changed over time from family-centric need to supplement family income to individualistic goals. Work became necessary for its own sake, so that career progression became an important target of women. (b) As families became more economically settled, consumerism started to emerge. This happened from the 1990s as globalisation introduced Indian society to Western life styles and allowed access to luxury goods. The economic motive of ensuring that the household reaches subsistence income evolved to satisfaction of Western-style consumerism. The need to earn more by moving up the organisational hierarchy became important to women and acceptable to their husbands. (c) The evolution in family structures minimised resistance to emancipation of women and shedding of the role of care provider. The increase in proportion of nuclear families has been noted in many studies. Simultaneously, there has been another shift in the nature of ties—from matrimonial families to maternal families. The increase in ties with the maternal family allowed women to seek help required during crises arising out of their working career without facing any criticism or resistance. Even in nuclear families, the socio-economic background of IT employees and the fact that women from their families have worked in earlier generations usually lowered resistance to women neglecting the family, by reducing expectations from working women.

As more people recognise the difficulties that a working woman faces in combining work and household duties, accompanied by a reduction in family structure (so that the number of possible critics within the household decline), the set of what is feasible expands. In terms of Fig. 3.6, the result of such changes is that the vertical line (H_i) shifts to the left, while the horizontal line (W_i) shifts upwards.

5.1.3 Social and Psychological Importance of Work

Apart from the less rigid expectations, another factor that is important in lowering the intensity of role conflict is the nature of the IT sector. The IT sector is a technological sector that is rapidly growing, high paying and highly competitive—so that working in the sector becomes a status symbol. The impact of prestige and high remuneration of IT workers may be analysed in terms of an intuitive model described by Sen (1990b) and referred in Chap. 1.

Sen argues that the household decisions are the outcome of cooperation between its members. But, as the interest of members may not match, there is also conflict between members. This results in bargaining between members to arrive at a mutually accepted choice regarding decisions. Obviously some outcomes will be favourable to a particular person, while others will be unfavourable to that person. Which outcome will be chosen will depend upon the bargaining power of the family member. In particular, the ability of the person to survive by walking out of the marriage will be a key determinant of the outcome. This is called fallback position of the agents.

Agarwal (1994) extends this argument by pointing out that the fallback position will depend, not only market forces, but upon social factors. In particular, how society shapes perceptions about the value of women's contributions to the family (contribution response) and how it shapes perceptions about the importance of women's well-being in the welfare function of the family is important. In a patriarchal society, typically, both will be low, reducing the bargaining power of women. This affects autonomy, agency and well-being of women.

The social status associated with a worker in the IT sector—particularly software engineers— along with the high level of education and remuneration makes it difficult to undervalue the economic contribution of women. In many cases, they are earning as much as their spouses. The extent of responsibility, interaction with foreign clients, undertaking of on-site assignments—makes the post glamorous in Indian society. The status of the women working in the IT sector are a far cry from those women working in traditional occupations like clerks, teaching and similar jobs. This gives them the confidence and bargaining strength needed to renegotiate their role in the family. As one respondent commented:

> No matter how much lip service ... people pay to equality, background, equal partnerships, at crucial moments it (remains) lip service... about independence, freedom to choose what you want to do, equal partnership, unless there is some extent of economic independence.

Another respondent said:

> Every one in my home ... gives me a lot of space ... a lot of freedom .... I have my own identity as a working woman. It feels so very good that you are productive... You are having your own social status. You are known not only through your husband's name but as an associate of TCS (Tata Consultancy Services). It gives a good feeling.

In-depth interviews reveal that education and economic independence provided by employment in a technical, high paying sector, are crucial in defining the role of respondents within the family. Respondents felt that employment allowed them to raise questions and issues that would otherwise not have been raised; it also enabled them to avoid questions that would otherwise have been raised:

> Economic freedom gives you a say. It is not deliberate, it gives you confidence ... you are more confident in sticking to what you think is correct. ... If you are economically independent then some questions will not rise at all—you have avoided those questions. If you are not, may be the issues are resolved in your favour, but the questions do come up.

For instance, one respondent mentioned that the confidence gained from working enabled her to go against her husband's wishes and insists on having a child. In contrast, a respondent, who had given up her work after marriage to devote time to her family, said that she felt 'empty headed ... useless ... I felt that I was not contributing anything to the family'.

It was not that the women are always participating in decision-making. In many cases respondents are so bogged down with their official responsibilities that they

Fig. 5.1 Satisficing in
Kolkata's IT sector

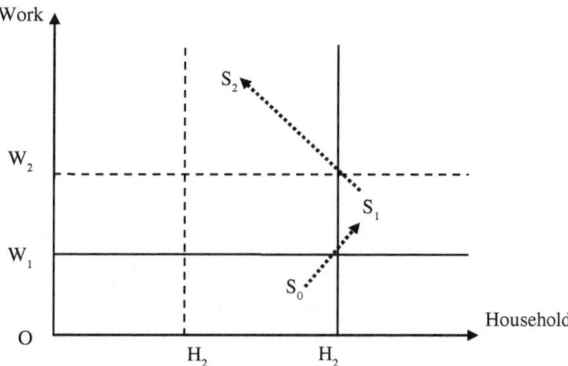

deliberately did not exercise this power—'If I am so busy in work, how can I take household decisions?' In spite of this, they value the feeling that they have the power to make their voice heard.

In brief, the initial entry of women into the labour market led to a change in outcome from S_0 to S_1. Given the social norms prevailing at that time—defining the feasible set by (H_1, V_1)—this movement was not particularly empowering; in fact women landed up with a dual burden. But, over time, social changes, like the increasing acceptability of women's work and the acknowledgment of women as individual entities, redefined the feasible set to one defined by (H_2, V_2). In the new situation, employment—particularly in a high-tech sector—and the consequent economic independence enhances the negotiating power of the women. As a result, women can bargain better with patriarchy and move 'deeper' and 'upward' into the satisfactory zone (Fig. 5.1) to a point like S_2.

5.2   Occupational Segregation

Researchers have pointed out that the existence of gender stereotyping in the IT and ITES sectors has led to occupational segregation within the industry. The belief that women find it difficult to acquire the 'hard skills' required in the hardware sector or display the aggressiveness and drive required from project consultants has led them to concentrate on software design. It has also been argued that difficulties faced by women employees in balancing work and home responsibilities often force them to opt for soft careers like quality assurance, testing and human relations. These sectors have fixed hours; another advantage is that on-site assignments and travelling can be avoided. This is observed not only in other developing countries (Wacjman and Lobb 2007), but also in New Zealand (Crump et al. 2007) and Germany (Ben 2007).

Now occupational segregation may be interpreted as the outcome of a deliberate attempt to balance work-home commitments through choice of career. Women who attach greater weight to family welfare opt for 'soft' careers (in departments like Quality Assurance and Human Relations). As these sectors have fixed hours and do not require travelling and on-site assignments, they enable respondents to look after family needs. At the other extreme, we have women with their focus set firmly on their career. Such women generally choose not to marry, and are prepared to accept off-site assignments, travel frequently, work long hours and so on. This group prefers demanding assignments like project consultancy. Most women, on the other hand, try to balance both work and home. These women accept only short term on-site and travelling assignments, delay having children to establish their reputation within the company to facilitate their comeback after a long layoff and rely on external (often hired) support system for household responsibilities. Such women are also dynamically adaptive. Over time, as their children grow older and require less care, their priorities change and are revised in favours of the office. Such women are willing to work in areas like software development, hardware research and other less 'soft' departments.

As pointed out previously, multiple equilibria are consistent with satisficing, and each agent makes her own career decision on the basis of individual circumstances. Respondents echo Hakim (1991, 1995, 1996a, 1996b) when they stress that occupational segregation is the outcome of deliberate occupational choices by women, based on their orientations:

> Women have to balance—and for balance they have to compromise (on their career). And the only thing that they can compromise is their sector… Different women are moulded differently. Some want to give more time to their work than to their marriage. Some women know they can balance their work and married life. It depends upon the women what they want to do.

To some extent, this may also explain the glass ceiling restricting entry of women into higher echelons of the IT industry. Both the first and third group of women workers are hampered by their focus on family and children, so that it is only the second group, forming a minority, which has the ability to break the glass ceiling.

5.3 Provisioning of Care Services

We had earlier referred to the pressures faced by working women who had to assume the dual role of a home-maker and income-earner. This is a problem that has been perennially faced by women. The first women workers from middle income families had entered the labour market solely to supplement family income. They were mainly clustered in lowly paid clerical jobs or in schools—occupations with fixed working hours. Further, the image of women as wife and mother, created by a patriarchal society, was deeply ingrained in their psyche. Bounded by 'socially imposed altruism',[1] these women workers therefore took upon the dual role of bread-earner and provider of care services.

---

[1] 'Social altruism' refers to the norm that assigns women greater responsibility for the care of dependents (Badgett et al. 2001).

Table 5.1 Regularity in Performing Household Tasks (percent)

Marital status	Household chore	Never	Occasionally	Always
Unmarried	Cooking	22.4	55.1	22.4
	Washing	20.0	54.0	26.0
	Dusting	18.4	59.2	22.4
Married	Cooking	9.1	55.1	22.7
	Washing	20.0	57.8	22.2
	Dusting	17.8	64.4	17.8

In the last two decades, as educated women became common, and the Indian economy became more integrated with the global economic system, women—particularly educated women from high middle income urban families—began to shift away from pink collar jobs (like teaching, secretarial assistance, receptionist, etc.) and competed with men for technical jobs. Employment is no longer linked to economic survival in such families; rather, it allows women to seek psychological satisfaction and sense of fulfilment outside the family. For instance, a software engineer said, 'It (my job) is so much a part of my identity ... I define myself to a very large extent on the basis of my work'. Similarly, another respondent said, 'I never had it in my mind that I will quit my job ... Whatever I have learned, if I can apply it in my practical life, that's the best thing'. Other respondents referred to the empowering effect of working.

The influences of globalisation and Western culture also left their imprint on the educated women workers in the Indian society. Not only did these give rise to gendered consumerism, but these also began to chip away at traditional patriarchal values. The earlier values based on the concept of personal care and service by household women were replaced by a more pragmatic, market-oriented mentality willing to substitute personal care by purchased services. This modified the traditional social altruism by still retaining women as persons responsible for the care and welfare of family members, but no longer making it obligatory on their part to fulfil this responsibility personally.

Consequently, though women are still the home makers, the way of doing it has changed so that the modified Game of Chicken (explained in Chap. 2) no longer holds. Our survey revealed that very few women undertook household chores themselves (Table 5.1). Only one out of five respondents cook, wash or dust on a regular basis. A significant proportion of such respondents are unmarried women, living as paying guests, or in rented accommodation. If only married women are considered, then also the proportion of women undertaking these tasks is about the same (20 %). This is contrary to what the Game of Chicken predicts in the presence of patriarchy, viz. that working women will perform household tasks.

The large pool of unemployed women from slums and from suburbs of Kolkata has been tapped by the middle and high income households to ensure that household chores are done without cutting into their own leisure time. In contrast to earlier contracts whereby such maidservants used to stay overnight or for the greater part of the day sequentially performing different household tasks, the system of *thike* has emerged in recent years. Under this system, part-time maid-servants work for two–three hours performing selective chores for the household. This allows the simultaneous provisioning of several tasks in the few hours before the wife leaves for work (or after her return from office) by the hiring of multiple *thike* maidservants.

The emergence of 'Centres' has also facilitated this process. Such centres hire out domestic workers on a per hour basis. This permits working women to hire such help for 10–12 h to perform the needed tasks. Affiliation of the helpers to centres guarantees their reliability and honesty. Further, as a helper becomes 'fixed' to a household, she becomes acquainted with its patterns and requirements. This is particularly important if the working woman has a child.

The availability of cheap domestic labour led to an important change in the role of women as care providers. As these maidservants supplied the labour to perform the household tasks, working women could shed the responsibility of performing the household chores personally. Instead, most of the respondents planned the tasks to be performed and supervised their execution. Since this reduced the drudgery, part of the supervisory role could even be shifted to the mother-in-law (if she resided in the same household).

In the case of absenteeism of such hired providers, temporary substitutes exist, helping to tide over emergencies. For instance, the system of 'home delivery' (of meals) has emerged in many areas of Kolkata. Similar to the *dabba* system in Mumbai, agencies supply cooked food to households. Many working women have reported that they use such services when their cook is absent, or when they are too tired to cook. Eating out has also become more common. As a software engineer remarked, 'If I don't feel like cooking, it's not that he (my husband) will cook; he will ask me to eat outside'.

In some nuclear families, sharing of household tasks has become accepted; some husbands help in case of household emergencies.[2] This is enough for respondents, who uniformly say 'I don't expect him to do (household chores) also', citing his lack of training as the reason—'you suddenly cannot change the demarcation inculcated from childhood'.

Such institutions are, of course, impersonal and are not based on altruism and a sense of serving the family. Nevertheless, they have become socially accepted over time. The gradual change in the family structure—the family became even smaller, consisting of just parents and children, with the grand-parents being gradually discarded and treated as part of an external support system[3]—has facilitated the

---

[2] Such emergencies arise when sudden visitors come, maidservants' absentee themselves and so on. In such situations, the introduction of electrical appliances facilitating household work becomes important in involving the husband in household chores. For instance, the husband can wash clothes when the maidservant has absented, or heat food simply by turning some knobs.

[3] For instance, this study found that in about 44 % households' cases there were no elderly persons within the family; only 14 % of the households had two elderly members. The family size is quite small, with 74 % of the families having less than 5 members.

substitution of personalised services provided by women members of the household by impersonal services provided by hired agents.

Even in households where in-laws reside with respondents, the shift away from traditional role of care giver and performer of household chores is accepted. This is partly because the mother-in-law was, in many cases, a working women and so able to understand the difficulties of balancing work and home. In quite a few cases, daughters were also working, and so in-laws understood work pressure faced by respondents and the reasons for them keeping late hours. The financial independence and status of respondents also reduced objections by in-laws. Finally, as respondents were often forced to leave housekeeping decisions to their mother-in-law, so that her authority within the household domain remains unchallenged, this reduced the scope for conflict between the two.

However, respondents reported, gender stereotyping of household roles still persists. An accepted practice is that husbands are responsible for 'outside the house' tasks related to financial matters. As one respondent remarked about her husband, justifying his failure to perform household tasks, 'He is otherwise extremely useful in the house—looking after banks and other financial matters'.

5.4 Child Care and Pregnancy

One problem with such purchased services is that the care providers cannot fully meet the emotional needs of children (Ferguson 1989). A respondent remarked that whenever the time came for her maidservant to leave, she felt tense in case any unexpected development prevented her from leaving at her scheduled time. Respondents reported that men colleagues are generally insensitive to child-related problems:

> There are people ... when you call up to say that you will be working from home because your maid hasn't turned up and you have to look after your daughter ... people don't say it but you feel it that men don't think ... realise that this is an issue—but it matters a lot to you. ... No one will say it why you are doing this ... because that is going against the code of conduct and also that would take away the liberated image from them.

An ITES employee said that when she left at 6 p.m, her colleagues perceived her to be slacking. The need to look after children is another reason for the reluctance to travel or accept long-term on-site assignments observed earlier, though companies generally accommodate such cases.

Pregnancy, therefore, has major implications for the working women. It has been observed by researchers (Mitter and Rowbotham 1995; COD 2004; Upadhya 2005) that pregnancy leads to a break in the career, and women are often unable to return to work thereafter. Respondents admitted that having children affected their careers as they are negatively evaluated during their leave period. To minimise the effect on their career, women preferred to establish themselves in their companies before having a child, so that they could return after about 2 years of leave (including unpaid leave). The 25-year old software engineer, Amrita, was aware that pregnancy and rearing up the child is demanding and will mark a difficult phase in her life.[4] Although she wanted a child very much and wanted to give the child 'the best of everything', she was equally determined not to sacrifice her career for her child. Other respondents spoke of the fulfilment in having and bringing up a child despite the immense pressure involved. IT women therefore plan their pregnancy carefully. For instance, Amrita had made up her mind to delay her pregnancy for at least 2–3 years, and then take a leave of about 2 years. This interval would enable her to accumulate enough leave, save enough to compensate for the temporary loss in income during her leave period and facilitate rejoining her company after her maternal leave by creating a good reputation. Once leave ends the situation becomes more complex. While some teams had a culture of working late hours—'When you rejoin, people expect you to swing back to work like they used to before … they expect these people to stay back till late at night'—others emphasised the output from the employee, allowing working mothers to leave at regular hours.

Working mothers generally rely on paid help, parents or in-laws in such cases. In Kolkata, neighbours are quite supportive. If meeting project deadlines prevent Ranjana, an employee in a company developing e-learning modules, from returning home before her maidservant leaves, her daughter is taken care by her neighbours. She also keeps in touch with their child during office hours through the telephone. Three-fourths of the women having children said that they always looked after their children themselves after returning home, while 11 % of such women kept aside their off-days for their children. We had also seen earlier that about 44 % of respondents spent their leisure hours in activities that may involve their children (visiting shopping malls, watching films, etc.). Respondents insist that this is deliberate—even those respondents whose households are run by their mothers-in-law find time to supervise their children's education and respond to their emotional needs. This is in keeping with the observation that women often incorporate the welfare of their children into their utility function (Sen 1990b).

At the same time, respondents do not sacrifice their careers for their child. Ranjana had to leave her daughter for 5 months to participate in an induction programme in Mumbai before joining her present company. She also mentioned that sometimes when her daughter rings her up she is busy. Although she realises that the information that her daughter wants to give may be of significance to the child, in some cases she does not answer the phone. Emotional deprivation of the child is accepted as a cost of careerism.

In all, respondents avail of better reproductive techniques to phase conception at a stage of their career when the perceived cost of withdrawal from the labour force is least. Initially, they look after the child taking leave. Subsequently, they

---

[4] Names of all respondents have been changed to protect their identity.

shift the responsibility of childcare to relatives and hired helps, but sacrifice their leisure hours to spend time with their children. This again constitutes an example of how respondents adapt their aspirations to attain a satisfactory outcome.

5.5 Satisficing Between Work and Household

Our analysis reveals that the status of women workers in Kolkata's IT sector is not as grim as portrayed in the printed media (see Appendix B). The pay and prospects of the IT industry had led them to join the sector. The prestige and status of working in the industry meant that their contribution to family welfare could not be ignored; simultaneously, the economic independence gave the women a sense of identity and confidence, thereby improving her fallback position within the family. Along with the evolution in family structure and changing expectations, this allowed the women to renegotiate their role within the family (Lee 2004) and modify patriarchal practices embedded within the family (Kelkar et al. 2002; Kelkar and Nathan 2002). While this has aided women to emerge from subjugation, they still face considerable constraints hindering their aspirations. The need to care for children personally, difficulties of relocation (even for short periods) and the pressure of working in an extremely demanding sector means that they have to adapt their aspirations and achieve a careful balance between their priorities, implying that the women satisfice.

The case of Amrita, a software engineer working in a domestic company, is a typical example of this trend. She works hard to establish her reputation in her company; this entails, on several occasions, late nights at office. She tries to compensate for this by spending time with her family during weekends. Frequent vacationing with her husband is also part of her 'balancing strategy'. Amrita is also averse to accepting on-site assignments as this will affect her work-home balance. She accepts the fact that this may affect her ratings marginally, but feels that this is a necessary cost of being able to spend time with husband, family and friends. However, her priorities are not static but adaptable over time; after 10–12 years of marriage, she is willing to prioritise her career over family and accept even long-term offshore assignments. Similar responses were obtained from young KPO (Knowledge Processing Outsourcing) employees like Priyanka and Indrani. Both stated unambiguously that they would refuse offshore assignments as their children needed their company, particularly at night. However, they were looking forward to accepting such assignments after their children had grown up so that they could see more of the world and be able to accelerate their career growth within the company.

Amrita's in-laws have accepted her careerism and are generally supportive. They realise that the specification of job timings has changed. While they expect that Amrita will return home by 6.30 p.m, they accept the fact that this is not always feasible in the new working environment. They retain reservations about her late nights, but Amrita's economic empowerment reduces the probability of outspoken resentment by her in-laws. They also appreciate the fact that she sets aside her weekends for them.

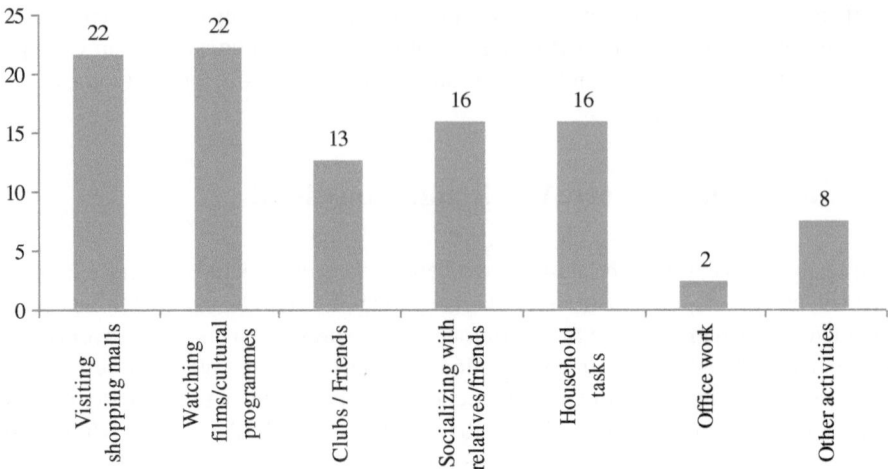

Fig. 5.2 Allocation of leisure hours by working women

Another example of satisficing is the way in which our sample spends their hours at home (Fig. 5.2). Only 20 % of respondents accorded first priority and 8 % accorded second priority to household duties in leisure allocation. On the other hand, activities in which the entire family takes part and enables the respondent to simultaneously undertake household tasks are becoming the preferred ways of spending leisure time. Examples of such multi-tasking activities are visiting shopping malls and watching films. These enable women to shop for grocery and other household items, have lunch/dinner and spend time with family members.

Overall, respondents were satisfied with the balance between work and home. It may be recalled that about 80 % of respondents (82 % of married workers) had reported that they were content with the current state of affairs.

5.6 Profiles

In addition to the questionnaire-based interviews we also undertook detailed unstructured interviews of 10 % of the respondents. Four of these profiles are described below.

5.6.1 Ranjana

Ranjana works in a major ITES company in Kolkata, involved in developing programmes and modules for e-learning. Ranjana belongs to a socio-economic class that is oriented towards a career. Her mother served as an important role model in her life. She taught her to be economically independent. Ranjana's mother was married to a patriarchal family while at school. She sold her ornaments to continue studying; completed her post graduation in humanities and got a job in a school—in the face of stiff opposition from her matrimonial home. This represents one of the rare instances of overt rebellion. However, not surprisingly, such overt resistance could not be sustained for long. After the birth of Ranjana, she felt that she was unable to continue her career and became a housewife.

Ranjana had completed her post graduation in English before joining a magazine as a journalist. After marriage she left her job and moved to Germany along with her husband, who was also in the same profession. There she became frustrated and depressed. She also felt guilty at not being able to contribute economically and turned reluctant on spending too much on articles of personal use. She decided to start freelancing. After returning to Kolkata, she found that freelancing was not given credit in the job market. In this phase, we can conceive Ranjana's choices being tightly restricted by labour market constraints; the resultant financial dependence weakened her ability to embark on a bargaining with the patriarchal system, so that she remained in the unsatisfactory (south-west) zone (see Fig. 3.6).

Although she conceived, Ranjana started preparing reports for an NGO (Non Governmental Organisation) and persisted with her freelancing activities. The part-time nature of her job meant that pregnancy did not seriously disturb her career. After her daughter was born, Ranjana applied to her present company and was accepted. However, her company insisted on a 5-month induction programme to be held in Mumbai. Initially Ranjana was reluctant to accept the job offer as they were living in a nuclear family and her daughter was new born. However, Ranjana's persistence in working garnered support from her husband, who insisted that she attend the induction programme—offering to take care of the child himself.

Work has now become an integral part of Ranjana's life. This has created a conflict between household and office duties. Ranjana has tried to balance her commitments to her office and home by hiring a girl from a 'centre'. Ranjana's maid comes at about 10 a.m and stays till 8 p.m. Further, Ranjana keeps tabs on her daughter by calling her. Her daughter also rings her up, if required. However, the pressure of office work creates problems. Ranjana said that she always became tense in the evenings as she had to return before her maidservant left. On quite a few occasions, she has to stay back to meet delivery deadlines. For instance, some time back, she had to work till 1 a.m for about a week. On occasions, her work finished at 3 a.m. Her husband is supportive and always takes care of the daughter when she is away. On a few occasions, however, both of them were swamped in work together. Ranjana's neighbours are supportive in such instances, and take care of her daughter.

Ranjana's is satisfied with her current position. The fact that she lives in a nuclear family implies the absence of any potential criticism from her in-laws. On the other hand, her husband is quite supportive. Networking relations also help her to overcome temporary crises like occasional late nights. Working provides her with a social status and enables the family to enjoy a high standard of living.

However, she feels guilty for having to depend on neighbours. Her feeling of guilt for not being able to spend enough time with her daughter is a part of her life. For instance, sometimes her daughter calls her after making a new dress for her doll. While this is a trivial issue, Ranjana realises it is important for her daughter. But at that point perhaps, she is unable to respond adequately as she is in the midst of an important meeting. The fractured identity, also reported by Mand (2008), is considered to be necessary costs of employment.

There are other problems faced by Ranjana. She has to get up at six in the morning no matter when she returns at night to prepare her daughter to go to school. She feels that her husband is supportive—he is prepared to operate the washing machine when there are too many clothes, or wash up the dishes when there are guests. Although, in general, he supports her and values the economic contribution made by Ranjana, he also sometimes gets annoyed with her late nights. Again adaptation is preferred to resistance as attempts to force her husband to play a greater role in household chores may alienate him so that he becomes less supportive. Such limits to the boundaries of her feasible set have been identified by Ranjana through a continuous process of negotiation with her spouse.

Interestingly, Ranjana realises that housewives have to work a lot, but feels that she can contribute in a worthwhile sense only if she contributes economically. This sense is encouraged by social interaction—after her return from Germany it was assumed that she was working and was asked what was her profession. The fact that she is helping to repay the housing loan taken to buy their flat means a lot to her. For her, work is both a means to increase consumption standards as well as create a sense of identity. She feels empowered and thinks that it is in her inter-actions with her colleagues that her sense of fulfilment and empowerment is best manifested.

Ranjana is an interesting example of an increasing group of working women, who form what Wilmott (1973) calls 'consumption partnerships' with their hus-bands (see Chap. 3). This choice is reflected in the family structure ideally geared to maximise consumption levels. She embodies the changed role of women within the family—from supplier of labour to a planning and supervisory role. However, she has not been able to change her attitude totally. The gender stereotyping of roles and equation of employment with contribution to the family persist in her psyche. She also thinks that looking after her daughter is her responsibility and feels guilty if her work prevents her from responding to her daughter's needs.

5.6.2 Geeta

Geeta is a worker in a KPO unit of a multi-national in Kolkata. She was born and brought up in New Delhi. She completed her post graduation degree in manage-ment, specialising in Finance. Her first job was teaching at a Technical Institute in

Delhi. Geeta married a KPO employee posted in Bangalore. In 2005, she shifted to Bangalore and decided to devote her time to her family. However, she felt 'useless … inefficient … empty headed'. Geeta's feeling that she was not contributing anything of worth to her family is interesting as it implies that she has accepted the conventional conception that only an earning member makes any significant contribution. When her husband left for China on a long-term assignment, she joined the BPO sector for a few months. However, her husband called her to join him in China. She again left her job and migrated to join her husband. Geeta's lack of financial independence placed her in a poor position to negotiate with patriarchy.

Her husband's next assignment was in Kolkata, where she joined her husband's company. Geeta had drifted into the IT sector because she could not find any teaching job in Bangalore, and remained in the IT sector in Kolkata as her husband's contacts enabled her to get a job easily. She is not really happy with her career as it does not match her educational profile. Geeta feels that Bangalore has a more cosmopolitan and professional environment than Kolkata. The workforce in Kolkata is composed predominantly of Bengalis, whom she finds rather insular and tending to communicate in the vernacular. This affects her ability to interact socially with her colleagues and develop networks that may provide her help during crises.

Geeta became pregnant in China. This was a planned pregnancy. Her husband did not want to bear the additional responsibility, and was rather nervous. However, he agreed to go on with her plans. Geeta joined her present post during her pregnancy and worked the full 9 months. After delivery, however, she had to take 6 months leave to look after her child. Fortunately, she had an extremely supportive Project Leader who gave her a laptop (even though she was not permitted to use one), and allowed her to initially work from home. Her hours were deliberately not monitored, permitting her to work for shorter hours. This aroused the jealousy of her colleagues, who were much less supportive. On the whole, however, her favourable work environment helped her to exercise her agency successfully. Her financial status was also important in giving her the self-confidence to stand up to her husband.

Geeta has to look after her child and cook. Her husband does not assist her in any household tasks. This is acceptable to her as she feels that it is not possible to modify the gender stereotyping inculcated in her husband since childhood. Her husband provides her with psychological support—that is all she expects from him. The work pressure is too much for her, and she is unable at times to balance her household needs and official responsibilities. She wants to leave the IT sector, but does not want to be unemployed.

Employment has given Geeta a sense of worth and self-confidence, particularly as she has broken into a non-traditional profession. She is less insecure and is able to 'put (her) side in front of others'. She said that she became less submissive after getting work and was able to renegotiate her role in household decision-making. For instance, she was able to convince her husband to have a child. However, she has been unable to break free of the gender stereotyping in household roles and 'social altruism'. While her husband agreed to have a child, he also made it clear that bringing up the child would be her responsibility. The fact that Geeta is working in a different state than her native state is also contributing to her problems. She lacks the support system of her parents, and is unable to interact with her neighbours and colleagues. This limits her social life, and has led to depression as well as hypertension. Geeta is also suffering from frequent stomach upsets and sleeping disorders, which are signs of anxiety and tension.

Geeta is clearly not in an optimum situation. Handicapped by lack of networks and an unfamiliar language and sociocultural environment, she has used her financial independence to test the limits of her agency. She has been able to satisfy her desire for motherhood; she realises that child caring will be difficult with only psychological support from her husband. But she is reluctant to risk this support by any overt resistance. Once again, this is a case of adapting to one's environment and obtaining to a situation which, rather than being the best, is satisfactory.

5.6.3 Subhra

Subhra is a technical manager in a MNC (Multi-national Corporation) software company. She is 31 years old, and has been married for about 7–8 years. She lives with her husband, son and in-laws. Her husband, too, is in the IT industry. He is an electrical engineer, working in a domestic software company.

Subhra always wanted to work. Her grandmother was widowed at the age of 31, and accepted a job offer in Raj Bhavan (Governor's Residence). Though the job was not highly remunerative, she stepped out of the confines of her well to do family and protected family life, in order to bring up her children all by herself. Her work exposed her to new experiences and acquaintances; it also gave her a say in family decision-making.

One of her aunts was another role model for Subhra. This aunt had married at the age of 15, and became a widow within a year. Though coming from a rural background, she plucked up courage to start working and bring up her child by herself.

The experiences of these persons made Subhra aware of the fact that the status of women, whatever be their family background, depends on her economic independence. In contrast to these women, another aunt, residing in USA, worked at home throughout the day, but felt that no one was recognising her contribution to the family.

Subhra feels that women need economic independence. She argued that even if a woman is educated or comes from an affluent family, even if her family accepts the notion of gender equality in decision-making, at crucial moments 'it all becomes lip service'. Work, according to Subhra, gave her the confidence of sticking to 'decisions that you think are correct'; she could also avoid questions that would otherwise have been raised. For instance, her work involves late nights. Her in-laws are not completely at ease with her late hours. However, the fact that she is working gives her the assurance to ignore the unspoken objections of her in-laws, thereby avoiding any conflict. As a result, over time, they have come to accept her late hours as natural. This may be interpreted as a case of covert resistance, leading to revision of family norms.

Subhra is very busy with her work. She does not find time to do household chores and be involved in the day-to-day running of the family. This, she acknowledges, is the responsibility of her mother-in-law. Her involvement in family decision-making is minimal. It is only with regard to the upbringing of her son that she exercises her control. She admits that her husband is supportive, and will help her in looking after their son if asked to. But he feels that childcare is still the exclusive responsibility of the mother. Nor does he help in tasks like cooking and washing, which are considered feminine activities. 'He is otherwise extremely useful in the house—looking after banks and other financial matters', said Subhra though he has been unable to break free from the stereotyped gendered division of household work. As a result, Subhra spends her leisure time with her son, and tries to keep on-site assignments to a minimum.

Subhra is quite happy with the prevailing situation. A possible reason for this is that directly challenging patriarchal norms could prove costly for her. It may give her greater decision-making power, but will also impose additional burden which will interfere with her work. More important than the actual outcome itself is the fact that her economic independence gives her the freedom to choose between outcomes. She does not have to act out of compulsion, but is guided by her choice. This gives her a subtle sense of empowerment.

Subhra could have reacted to her in-laws objections to working late by resisting overtly and shifting to a nuclear family. However, her deliberate ignoring of such disapproval enabled her to avoid confrontation with her in-laws. She has also given up her decision-making power with respect to household decisions. These proved useful in the case of bringing up her child. She is one of the few respondents who are able to access family support with respect to childcare. The fractured identity that other respondents suffer was not observed for Subhra. Again, her actions after marriage represent a sequential movement towards a satisfactory outcome.

5.6.4 Amrita

Amrita is a 25 years old software engineer in a major domestic software company. After completing her graduation, she was selected by State Bank of India through a campus interview. Initially she was posted to Gauhati, before being transferred to Shillong. While working for State Bank, she met her future husband and started going out with him. Amrita realised that working in two different sectors would create problems in her marital life. Despite this realisation, she never thought of stopping work. Instead, she applied to her husband's company for a job and was accepted. This was very convenient for her as the company was located near her matrimonial home.

While speaking to us, Amrita emphasised that she had never contemplated giving up her job. She referred to the sense of fulfilment and gratification obtained from the practical application of her knowledge and skills. Meeting different people in her working environment increased her awareness and made her more confident. Work also gave her an identity distinct from that of her husband—the fact that she was working in a major IT company increased her prestige and status in her family and friend circle. At home, it enabled her to carve out a personal space for herself.

Economic motives were also important. She believed that a double income was necessary to maintain the standard of living that her family was accustomed to. She also referred to the fact that economic empowerment enabled her to satisfy her gendered consumerism. Work also allowed her to purchase care services instead of engaging in personal labour within the home environment. Amrita pointed out that a working woman faces multiple and conflicting objectives—she has to look after her children, spend time with her husband and socialise with in-laws, relatives and friends, while simultaneously trying to establish herself in her office. She repeatedly emphasised the need to balance these objectives and plan her career accordingly, based on priorities accorded to these objectives.

For instance, although she had married at the age of 23 years, she was initially planning to accord priority to her career. She mentioned that after 2 or 3 years of marriage she would start planning her pregnancy. Amrita was fully aware of the fact that pregnancy and rearing up the child would be demanding and mark a difficult phase in her life. Although she wanted a child very much and give the child 'the best of everything', she was also determined not to sacrifice her career for her child. Accordingly, she had made up her mind to delay her pregnancy for at least 2–3 years, and then take a leave of about 2 years (of which the major part would be unpaid leave). It was partly because of this fact that she wanted time to establish herself in her company before contemplating pregnancy. On the one hand, she would be able to save enough to compensate for the temporary loss in income during her leave period; on the other hand, it would facilitate rejoining her company after her maternal leave by creating a good reputation.

Amrita was therefore working hard to establish her reputation in her company. This entailed, on occasions, late nights at office. She tried to compensate for this by spending time with her family during weekends. The fact that her husband was also in the IT sector helped her. Frequent vacationing with her husband is also part of her 'balancing strategy'. She is also averse to accepting on-site assignments as this will affect her work-home balance. She accepts the fact that this may affect her ratings marginally, but feels that this is a necessary cost of being able to spend time with husband, family and friends. However, later on, after 10–12 years of marriage, she is willing to prioritise her career over family and accept even long-term on-site assignments.

In the immediate present, her in-laws have accepted her careerism and are generally supportive. They realise that the specification of job timings has changed. Women are no longer confined to occupations involving fixed hours, but have to work in shifts and keep late nights while working in the corporate sector. While they expect that Amrita will return home by 6.30 p.m, they accept the fact that this is not always feasible in the new working environment. While they have reservations about her late nights, Amrita realises that this is a problem that must be faced. She devotes her weekends to her family and her in-laws. Her economic empowerment also reduces the probability of outspoken resentment by her in-laws.

Overall, Amrita's life and career are characterised by the need to balance work and home. Her family's attitude is supportive, so that her feasible set is more in the north-west quadrant of the diagram than other respondents. Her own actions of overt submission to her in-laws, while maintaining her right to work and stay out for late hours, have also helped her to define a favourable feasible set. Again, confrontation will destabilise family relations that may affect her adversely subsequently—particular after she has a child. Amrita is aware that, in the future, she will have to face different challenges and expectations—spending time with her husband, socializing with in-laws, relatives and friends and (in the future) bringing up her child. She realises that maintaining such a balance is difficult, but is necessary. Hence, she is attempting to adjust her career and home life to obtain a satisfactory outcome.

5.6.5 Indrani

Indrani is a Commerce graduate who subsequently completed her MBA in Finance from Institute of Chartered Financial Analysts of India Business School. She joined as Administrator in a MNC in 2007; in 2012, she was promoted to Assistant Manager of IT (Operations).

Indrani's father worked in a bank, while her mother was, in Indrani's words, 'a home-maker'. When asked about her choice of words, Indrani stressed on the important role that her mother played in her family—even though she was not paid—without receiving her due credit. In 2010, she married a West Bengal Civil Service officer. Her father-in-law was also a bank employee, while her mother-in-law was a housewife. However, the present generation in her matrimonial family had several women who worked. As a result, her in-laws quite understood about her late nights and inability to perform household chores due to work pressure. On occasions, they do react to her mood—particularly when she gets upset and tensed due to excessive work pressure; but such occasions are rare.

When asked about reasons for working, Indrani identified two reasons. First, she argued, education gave her an ability and skill; working enabled her to utilise this skill and justified her education. Second, in current times, double income was necessary to maintain a reasonable standard of living and bring up the family. This indicated that she thought of the family as both a consumption and investment unit.

Indrani has to bear substantial family responsibilities. While the daily tasks are performed by paid care providers, she does a fair amount of washing, cleaning and cooking in the weekends. Her husband is posted in Murshidabad, and returns only on weekends. Even during these visits he has to either finish his office work or undertake outside home chores. Support from her husband, therefore, is minimal.

Indrani has a son aged 13 months. While she has hired an ayah to look after the child, she spends her leisure time with him. Her son gives her a lot of problems as he does not sleep well at night. This has affected her health. Nevertheless, Indrani realises, rejoining work after a long break will affect her career options and career growth; this is why she persisted working despite these problems. Currently, she is on a rotational shift, which creates further adjustment problems. However, she is lucky in the sense that her team consists of several working mothers so that she receives sympathy and support during crisis. The relation between Indrani and her colleagues is a case of networks between women in a similar situation helping them to face crises.

Indrani reported that her mother-in-law takes most of the household decisions. This has resulted in an undercurrent of tension as Indrani wanted a greater say in household affairs. However, she is aware that starting a conflict with her in-laws is not feasible. She cited work pressure, rotating shifts and absence of husband as factors constraining her desire for greater say in the household domain. Indrani is fully aware that without her mother-in-law's support she will not be able to maintain a home and bring up her child, and is willing to accept her lack of autonomy as a necessary cost. Consequently, she does not want to challenge her mother-in-law, preferring to behave strategically in the face of situational realities. For instance, if her work pressure leads to any work-home conflict, Indrani prefers to communicate with her in-laws to make them appreciate her problem and win over their approval.

Indrani's case is an instance of what was referred to as 'structured individuation' (Roberts 1994) in Chap. 3. She is neither passively moving towards goals imposed upon her by society and family, nor is she embarking on a career of overt resistance and protest. Rather, she is adapting her aspirations in the light of structural constraints on her agency and empowerment and trying to balance multiple objectives through a satisficing choice.

Regarding her work-home jugglery, she insists that she is balancing both her family needs and work pressure on a daily basis—'Balancing to amra korchi'. At some points, she prioritises her work; subsequently, she makes up the loss to her family by focusing on them. But, Indrani points out, in some cases the choice faced may be a once and for all choice. In such cases, she realises that she will have to sacrifice her work concerns in the short run. Refusing offshore assignments is one example of such a sacrifice. So far, Indrani has not been offered any offshore assignment. If she is offered any such assignment, Indrani claimed, she would refuse such assignments unless they were for less than a month. She is aware that this will slow her career growth, but she insisted that her son would miss her, particularly at night. She is sure that she will regret this sacrifice, but this will be partially compensated by availing of such offer in the future, when her child has grown up sufficiently. When we asked Indrani whether her choice to prioritise her child over her career was due to the need to satisfy societal norms, she was quick to disagree and stress that it was a conscious choice on her part.

5.6.6 Priyanka

Priyanka is employed in the Operations unit of a major KPO company with a branch in Kolkata. She has joined the company in 2013.

Priyanka comes from a family with a history of working women. Her parents were both post graduates in Business Administration and had jointly set up an entrepreneurial unit. Priyanka completed her graduation in Social Sciences and enrolled in the MBA (Master of Business Administration) programme in a private company. After completing her education, Priyanka left Kolkata to join, initially, a marketing research company and then an ITES firm in Delhi. Her reasons for working were financial independence and '*barite thakte* boring *lage*' (it is boring to stay at home).

In 2008, she married. Her husband was working in Delhi. They lived a bachelor's existence initially—hardly cooking, but eating out most of the days. Then, in 2010, her husband came to Kolkata to join a new firm. Around this time, she also conceived. Priyanka initially took maternity leave and returned to Kolkata, but when her husband left Delhi, she resigned from her Delhi job. After her child had crossed one year, Priyanka resumed working. Initially she joined a brokerage company. The work pressure and environment was not conducive; as a result she shifted to her present job.

Priyanka's son is looked after by a domestic help, working for 12 h. Her work ends at 5:30 p.m, and she leaves nearby. Moreover, working hours are flexible, with supportive team members helping her in case of crises. This eases her child caring concerns. On instances, when work pressure delays her return, her child is looked after by her in-laws. Nevertheless, Priyanka reported that her son reacts to such late returns, becoming very upset—'*sare attay ma–ma kore othe*' (cries for his mother at 8:30 p.m).

Her mother-in-law is very supportive and understanding. This is partly because she herself had worked as a school teacher and partly because her own daughter, employed in a similar job, works for even more odd hours. She does not complain that Priyanka does not cook or performs other household chores during weekdays. On weekends she does some cooking, but not on a regularly basis.

Priyanka commented that balancing work and home was very exhausting, particularly in the brokerage company. In contrast, such balance is easier to achieve in her current job. The comfortable work environment of her office reduced the physical strain. The support of her team members, mentioned earlier, is also important in this context. She enjoys work, finds fulfilment in her assignments and intends to stay on in this sector—'there is no better situation for a working woman'.

However, she realises that she cannot maximise her satisfaction with respect to *both* work and home. In some cases, she sacrifices her career for her family; on other occasions, work is prioritised over family concerns. Currently, as her son is still very young, the former happens commonly. She is quick to point out that the situation is not symmetric so far as her husband is concerned—'Husband (job) opportunity *pele chole jabe, kintu aami parbo na'* (if my husband gets an opportunity then he will leave, but I cannot do so). But this is not necessarily lack of empowerment. She feels that her choice is because of her 'emotional attach-ment—*keu atkato na.* (The choice) individual to individual vary *kore* … (It is a matter of) free choice, not compulsion' (the choice is because of my emotional attachments to my son, not because any one will stop me. However, the choice varies across individuals. In my case it is a matter of free choice and not due to any compulsion).

5.7 Summing Up

The analysis of survey responses and profiles reveals that household responsibil-ities prevent women from maximising their career growth. Respondents regret this sacrifice, but stress that this is a conscious choice that is not forced upon them by their family. They also plan to reprioritise their goals and focus more on their career advancement when their child grows up. In all, respondents try to balance different aspects of their life keeping in mind their contextual constraints; it also appears that they are content with the balance attained. This indicates that, rather than either maximising their career growth or subordinating their career to household, women workers satisfice.

References

Agarwal, B. (1994). *A field of one's own: Gender and land rights in South Asia.* Cambridge: New Delhi.

Badgett, M., Lee, V., & Folbre, N. (2001). Gender norms and economic outcomes. In M. F. Loutfi (Ed.), *Women, gender and work: What is equality, and how do we get there?* (pp. 327–341). Geneva: ILO.

Basu, A. M., & Amin, S. (2000). Conditioning factors for fertility decline in Bengal: History, language identity, and openness to innovations. *Population Development Review, 26,* 761–794.

Ben, Esther Ruiz. (2007). Defining expertise in software development while doing gender. *Gender, Work and Organization, 14*(4), 312–332.

Bhattacharya, M. (2005). Culture. In J. Bagchi (Ed.), *The changing status of women in West Bengal: 1970–2000. The challenge ahead.* New Delhi: Sage Publishers.

Centre for Organization Development. (2004). Final report on women in information technology. Report submitted to Department of Women & Child, Ministry of Human Resource Development, Government of India, Hyderabad.

Crump, B. J., Logan, K. A., & McIlroy, A. (2007). Does gender still matter? A study of the views of women in the ICT industry in New Zealand. *Gender, Work and Organization, 14*(4), 349–370.

Ferguson, A. (1989). *Blood at the root: Motherhood, sexuality and male dominance.* London: Pandora Press.

Hakim, C. (1991). Grateful slaves and self made women: Fact and fantasy in women's work orientation. *European Sociological Review, 7*(2), 101–121.

Hakim, C. (1995). Five feminist myths about women's employment. *British Journal of Sociology, 46*(3), 429–455.

Hakim, C. (1996a). The sexual division of labor and women's heterogeneity. *British Journal of Sociology, 47*(1), 178–188.

Hakim, C. (1996b). *Key issues in women's work: Female heterogeneity and the polarization of women's employment.* London: Athlone.

Kelkar, G., & Nathan, D. (2002). Gender relations and technological change in Asia. *Current Sociology, 50*(3), 427–441.

Kelkar, G., Shreshtha, G., & Veena, N. (2002). IT industry and women's agency. *Gender, Technology and Development, 6*(1), 63–84.

Lee, J. C. (2004). Access, self-image and empowerment: Computer training for women entrepreneurs in Costa Rica. *Gender Technology and Development, 6*(1), 63–84.

Mand, K. (2008). Marriage and migration through the life course: Experiences of widowhood, separation and divorce amongst transnational Sikh women. In R. Patriwala & P. Uberoi (Eds.), *Marriage, migration and gender* (pp. 286–302). New Delhi: Sage.

Mies, M. (1986). *Patriarchy and accumulation on a world scale.* London: Zed Press.

Mitter, S., & Rowbotham, S. (Eds.). (1995). *Women encounter technology: changing patterns of employment in the third world.* New York: Routledge.

Sen, A. K. (1990). Gender and co-operative conflicts. In I. Tinker (Ed.), *Persistent inequalities: Women and world development* (pp. 129–149). New York: Oxford University Press.

Upadhya, C. (2005). Gender issues in the Indian software outsourcing industry. In A. Gurumurthy, P. J. Singh, A. Mundkur, & M. Swamy (Eds.), *Gender in the information society: Emerging issues* (pp. 74–84). New Delhi: UNDP-AIDP & Elsevier.

Wajcman, J., & Pham Lobb, L. A. (2007). The gender relations of software work in Vietnam. *Gender, Technology and Development, 11*(1), 1–26.

Young, M., & Willmott, P. (1973). *The symmetrical family.* London: Routledge & Kegan Paul.

Chapter 6
Work, Satisficing and Agency

Abstract The final chapter summarises the main findings of the study and critically examines the genuineness of the empowerment claimed by the respondents.

Keyword Empowerment

6.1 An Overview

The importance of involving women in development by encouraging their participation in the labour market has been widely recognised by researchers, activists and policy makers. However, the process of integrating women in the development process and its implications for women's agency has remained a contentious issue. Feminist researchers like Mies (1986) have argued that capitalist relations existing in the economy and patriarchal relations existing within the household are integrated into one synergistic system creating bi-polarism within both spheres—the economic sphere and the household sphere. In both domains, we have two classes—one exploiting, and the other being exploited. Extending classical Marxist theory, Mies argues that the entry of women into the labour market has not empowered them because the patriarchal relations that demarcates them as the exploited class within the household domain, spills over to the economic domain and forces them to remain in the ranks of exploited in this domain also. In fact, the patriarchal relations and norms subjugating women socially are used by economic forces to exploit them economically also. Pearson and Elsom's (1981) analysis of women workers in the export-based industries of South-east Asia and Banerjee's (1985, 1991, 1992) analysis of women workers in Kolkata's informal sector are important studies in this tradition. These studies have argued that the involvement of women from low income households in the labour market does not have any positive effect on their socio-economic status.

But, can we generalise this analysis to the whole of society? As Lim (1990) points out, some Marxist writers base their conclusions on extreme cases and generalise them to the entire society and to all countries. The binary view of

Z. Husain and M. Dutta, *Women in Kolkata's IT Sector*,
SpringerBriefs in Sociology, DOI: 10.1007/978-81-322-1593-6_6,
© The Author(s) 2014

women as marginalised and passive agents has been questioned in recent years by feminist researchers. Instead, these writers argue, women try to utilise their limited resources to engage on a continuous bargaining with the patriarchal system. Instead of outright resistance, which may threaten their limited domains of authority and affect their economic security, women prefer to rely on covert means of resistance and subversion of the dominant ideology to create space for greater exercise of their agency and increase their autonomy. The Marxist approach suggests that, while patriarchy allowed women to enter the labour force to supplement household income without compromising their gender role as provider of care services, women may use the windows of opportunity provided by employment to improve their status within the household and create space for their agency. In this study, we argue that such sequential improvement in status may be conceived in terms of Simon's satisficing model.

Focusing on a specific section of the steadily growing community of urban educated women, consisting of women workers in the IT sector, we examine how these women combine their work and household responsibilities. We argue that women are able to exercise agency in attaining a trade-off between these two activities. How they do so was described in Chap. 5.

6.2 Constrained Agency

In West Bengal, women had, for a long time, been denied education. It was only in the ninetieth century that social reformers campaigned for educating women. Even this demand had its limitations, as the motive was solely to ensure that women would be better equipped to be companions to their husbands and be able to bring up their children (Mies 1986; Mukhopadhyay and Seymour 1994). After Partition, inflation and economic distress forced the entry of women from middle class families into the labour market. Since this was again a society-imposed decision, it did not lead to any genuine empowerment in the short run. In the second-generation, particularly with globalisation changing the sociocultural environment of the country, women's education spread and its motives changed drastically. Simultaneously, motives for entering the labour market became more self-centred, consumption-oriented and were a result of conscious decision-making by the women concerned. The legitimisation of the role of women as workers led to changing expectations from them with regard to their traditional role as care provider. Such changes provided women workers with scope to exercise their agency, as may be seen from an analysis of women workers in Kolkata's IT sector.

Our survey reveals that women workers in Kolkata's IT sector belong to an exclusive socio-economic category—urban-based, middle income, English-speaking and educated families. As a result their motivations for seeking employment, attitudes towards life and family, and actions are different from the low income women workers (Noronha and D'Cruz 2008). Similarly, the constraints that they face at work and at home are unique to themselves (Drew et al. 2003).

Such constraints restrict the freedom of the women in many ways and force her to adapt her aspirations to the structured realities created by social and workplace institutions. Starting from their choice of occupation, their job decisions, allocation of leisure time, pattern of spending after office hours—all the choices of these women workers represent a dynamic adjustment of aspirations to structural realities. Although such realities may constrain the actions and choices of women in various ways, they do not prevent her from exercising her agency. Rather, the agency is demonstrated in their ability to balance conflicting situations to achieve a more or less satisfactory outcome. Such adaptation of aspirations, we argue, may be conceptualised in terms of a satisficing framework.

6.2.1 Motives for Working

The women workers in the Mexican *maquiladoras*, in the semiconductor industries of East Asia, and in the informal sector of India all come from poor households struggling to eke out a living. The women are allowed to violate traditional social norms and enter the labour market out of economic necessity. In other words, economic motivations relating to survival underlies the employment of these women workers.

In contrast, studies of working women in developed economies have noted the importance of non-economic motivations underlying the decision to work. A similar pattern of behaviour is also observed among the respondents of our survey. The primary motives underlying the decision of respondents to work are to create a personal space (Kenny 1978) and to support their consumerist lifestyles (Young and Wilmott 1973). The latter has an important implication. Since their consumerism often has externalities for other family members—when it leads to the purchase of durable consumer goods—objecting to women's work becomes costlier.

6.2.2 Care Services and Work–Family Balance

The entry of women into the labour market breaks down the gendered division of labour and creates a vacuum within the household. While housewives can perform household chores during the day time, working women cannot. One possibility, as we have seen, is to hire persons who will undertake such jobs. This option is feasible in Asian countries, where cheap female labour is available. In countries characterised by shortage of domestic help, or if the household cannot bear the financial burden of hiring such services, the woman has to perform these tasks herself before or after office hours—originating in the practice of the double shift. However, the problem becomes more serious in the case of child care. The reason is that child care has to be provided round the clock. The need to balance work and the provisioning of such care services while achieving their individual aspirations emerge as a major constraint for working women. Such constraints may operate in two spheres—workplace and home.

In general, the constraints originating in the male-dominated workplace culture, one of the primary determinants of the extent to which work–household balance may be attained, are more rigid. Although companies offer flexible working hours or superiors may be sympathetic, attitude of superiors and colleagues towards sacrificing work hours to cope with household pressure is not always very supportive. Refusal to accept offshore assignments affects promotion, creating glass ceiling for women. Even maternity leave affects ratings—with women getting negative or average ratings during the leave period.[1]

In such cases, women tend to prioritise their household concerns over office concerns, even at the cost of their career growth. The objective of such submission to patriarchy is to remove possible long-term resistance of in-laws and husband and get them accustomed to the implications of working in the IT sector (late nights, assignments during off-days, etc.). The process of lowering resistance is facilitated by the fact that most of the respondents are from families where the concept of working women is not new. Similarly, they are marrying into families where working women have become a second-generation phenomenon. As a result, matrimonial families accept that it may not be feasible for the working daughter-in-law to provide personal care services. In many cases, the respondent resides in nuclear families so that question of conforming to traditional behavioural norms becomes a trivial issue. Such flexibility permits working women to shift away from a traditional caring and family oriented role, and rely more upon purchasing care services. Instead of personally undertaking household tasks, women now assume a planning and supervisory role.

In case of important assignments, women attempt to protect career concerns by working extra hard on days in which they do not have any pressure from home. Realising that child caring will impose extra pressure, women delay pregnancy till their reputation is sufficiently established in their company. Adverse rating (during leave) and reduced commitment to work does not, therefore, have any serious long-term impact on their career. Further, she utilises the support of her in-laws, or (in the case of nuclear families) her husband or neighbours in case of excessive work pressure. Two factors facilitate social acceptance of the shift in role of working women—the economic independence from working in the high-paying IT sector, and the fact that this sector is a technical non-traditional sector. If working in the IT sector increases the importance of the respondent in terms of her economic contribution to the family, the glamour and prestige of being associated in a frontier industry helps her to carve out her own niche within the family.

Over time the family situation changes. The child grows up and is better able to take care of itself; in-laws, too, grow older and provide more space to their

---

[1] It is therefore necessary to bring about a radical change in the work structure, ethos and practices of current workplace culture to facilitate a more favourable work–household balance. Possible alternatives, based on practices followed in European Union countries, are reviewed in Redmond et al. (2006).

daughters-in-law. In many cases, there may be a split to nuclear households. All these provide space to the women on the household front. They are now able to change their priorities and focus more on work.

6.2.3 Child Care

The only domain in which women prefer to retain control is with respect to upbringing of the child. Realising that pregnancy will affect their careerism, women schedule their pregnancy to occur after having established their reputation as a reliable and committed worker. Such a schedule minimises the adverse effects of career breaks. In the initial phases, when the child is too young to take care of themselves, women prioritise their commitment towards the infant; they use flexible hours and avoid offshore assignments to provide their child with the necessary care services and psychological support. Even household activities not related to the child are planned to enable women to spend time with their children. Over time, there is a reordering of priorities, with the focus shifting back towards work and career. Although, this sort of planning does produce nonlinearity's in their working career, the costs are considered unavoidable and more than compensated by the sense of fulfilment from bringing up the child. A woman-respondent admitted that bringing up a child was very tough and involved a lot of sacrifices; but, in the end, 'every woman will say that it was worth it'.

6.3 Comparing Results

The findings of this study contrast with the findings of other studies of women workers in the IT sector. While earlier studies had observed, on lines similar to that of the Marxist feminist writers, that women were exploited both at home and office. On the other hand, the economic independence of the women workers in Kolkata's IT sector provides them with the agency to make choices. The women workers exercise this agency to carefully balance multiple, competing objectives in the work–home sphere and obtain a satisficing solution.

Interviews with women workers revealed that all these women had aspirations. But they were also aware of their situational realities that made attempts to attain all such aspirations costly. Consequently, women workers modified their aspirations to their context, rather than embark on a head on challenge of the constraints, and try to balance their choices over the long run. Such a strategy is deliberate and a result of a conscious process of decision-making.

This raises the question: why do the results differ from the findings of feminist writers reviewed in Chap. 2. There are two reasons for the variation in findings.

The first reason is a reluctance to conceptualise women as free agents capable of making choices in any domain. Women are viewed as grateful slaves, passively accepting decisions made by male authority figures in the domain of both work and home. To what extent this is a valid image for women is doubtful. For instance, even the poor and uneducated women working in the export-based industries had the capacity of revolting. Such resistances may assume overt form, as in the militant trade unionism of Korean women in the 1970s and 1980s—at a time when male workers were docile. Or it may take covert forms as mocking absent supervisors, deliberately slowing down production. It may also take symbolic forms like ghostly possession and mass hysteria.

Even in the household domain, women have some areas of exclusive control. Women can exercise control and even discrimination in several decisions. For instance, women distribute food between household members and they can exercise some autonomy to subvert norms determining allocation of food pieces between members (Harriss 1995). The feminist literature reviewed in Chap. 3 provides further instances of such agency. In this context, particularly given the level of education of respondents, the conceptualisation of women as passive slaves seems somewhat far-fetched.

Second, there are differences in both the historical background and economic context. Historical changes in the sociocultural sphere had led to a redefining of the image of women and a corresponding change in expectations from them. The changes in image of women and expectations from them reduced the intensity of role conflict. Similarly, the economic context—the socio-economic background of the respondents, the nature of the job, the availability of substitute care services—all these factors either remoulded expectations or widened the alternatives available. If we replace the assumption of women as passive agents with the assumption of budding decision-maker, seeking to identify the constraints on her agency and testing the limits of her freedom, then the widened choice set and flexible expectations can be utilised by these women to enhance their agency.

Thus, there is need to shed the Marxist pessimism about the failure of employment to ensure economically independence of women. The Marxist works had rightly pointed out that work is not a sufficient condition for empowerment. But instead of equating overt submission and lack of resistance with a lack of agency, it is necessary to explore into the complexities of gendered space more critically. This will help in understanding more accurately the linkages between work and empowerment, and how the work–home conflict is dealt with by women.

6.4 How Genuine is this Empowerment?

In conclusion, we argue that the establishment and growth of the IT sector in Kolkata has created opportunities for educated urban women from affluent households to participate in economic growth process of the region. The hi-tech nature of the IT sector and the high salary structure in the IT companies makes such employment prestigious. In the work sphere the effect on agency is complex. Although the IT sector has been the instrument through which these women have increased their agency, work relations in the sector has remained male-centric and still does not permit scope for continuous career development of women.

In the household sphere, the status and prestige of being involved in the IT sector has three implications. Workers can satisfy their own and their family's consumerism, reducing social resistance to their employment and allowing them to create a space for themselves. Such space has been utilised by women to carve out their destiny and express their own identity. Work, respondents argue, have empowered them and increased their sense of agency—even though they do not always attain their desired goals, or even try to exercise their autonomy.

But are these changes indicative of genuine empowerment of women? Have their agencies really been enhanced, or is it a mirage sugar-coated by the gendered consumerism that women can afford? Walby (1997) points out that for women, choices about how to balance work and caring responsibilities are *always* restricted, no matter what their circumstances, due to the fact that they have not generally been in powerful positions to determine the structures that govern choice.

For instance, there has always been a division of labour between the affluent men and women, with the former performing the role of breadearner and the latter the role of housemaker and caregiver. Over time, social changes have led to a disintegration of this bi-polar outcome. The confines binding women to the home have broken down, offering them a choice between work and home. The burden emerging from the contradictory nature of work and home, nonetheless, rests solely on women. Whether this really represents a choice is debatable. Proctor and Padfield (1998) argue that for choice to be meaningful, work and family must be socially organised to permit either one or both to be experienced, as is the every day experience of men in society.

When we raised this issue before respondents, they admitted the validity of this proposition. They referred to the social limits on their aspirations and choices, the asymmetrical gender relations still persisting at home and work. Respondents complained about the long hours of monotonous work. Respondents also suffer from fractured identities, as is evident from their guilt in not giving enough time to their family and particularly to their child. In spite of this, respondents also pointed out that the outcomes now are not hoisted on the respondents by a patriarchal family taking advantage of the employment opportunities created by globalisation, but are deliberate choices made by the women. As one respondent remarked, 'Earlier it was not the girl's choice. They had to do what their family allowed'.

Technically, educated women attempt a static and inter-temporal balancing of the work–household concerns—focusing on household initially, followed by the child and then the career. They recognise that such balancing does not maximise career growths; nor does it satisfy the psychological needs of children. Despite this, most respondents reported that they were satisfied with this outcome as this was the best they could do, given their circumstances. Even Geeta, who did not seem very happy, understands that she does not have a better option, and finds some sort of fulfilment in her motherhood.

On the other hand, some women opt for softer fixed hour jobs. Such women prioritise household (and child care) concerns over work. Given the nature of their assignments, this is feasible. Our respondents also reported that some women, admittedly rare, were devoted to their career. Such women either avoided marrying or having children, or were comfortable with hiring care services to perform these services.

An ongoing survey of women from middle income households of Kolkata currently being undertaken by us indicates that Hakim may have been right when she claimed that women could be classified into three groups—having a long-term commitment towards the family, or towards her career, or drifting between the two, and wanting both.[2] What is important about these three sets of women is that their decisions are, to a major extent, formed at an early stage, through their educational choices. Subsequently, after marriage, they persist with their choice or switch over to a second best option (like Ranjana or Geeta). Also important is the fact that the respondents specifically expressed their satisfaction with the work–home balance attained; moreover, majority of respondents voiced their intention to remain in the IT sector till retirement (Chap. 4). These indicate their satisfaction with their current balance.

To conclude, although society may still circumscribe their choice set, the women workers in Kolkata's IT sector have obtained the agency to choose between focusing on home, balancing work and home, and opting for careerism. The decision to choose the second option is therefore a deliberate one. In a lecture delivered in 1998,[3] Amartya Sen examined the relationship between freedom and the process of arriving at an outcome. He considered a bliss point (a point where welfare is maximised) that was reached through the operation of market forces and freedom of the agent to choose an outcome. Sen's assumed that the state could identify this point and allocated resources resulting in the individual ending up in the earlier bliss point. Sen's question was: Are the two outcomes (both yielding the same level of welfare) same? He argued that in the second situation the absence of freedom to choose resulted in a qualitative loss so that the second point is necessarily inferior.

The capability approach would argue that that the ability of the women workers to choose between options is an indication of freedom and agency—even though the women end up in the same equilibrium as when society imposes the choice. During our interviews, several respondents emphasized that they were so bogged down with office work and responsibilities that they did not want to shoulder the burden of decision-making at home also. It was not true that working women were not allowed to participate in household decisions. As Subhra points out (see Chap. 5) her voice is heard, her opinions matter. It is her deliberate choice not to exercise her autonomy except with decisions relating to her son. Respondents

---

[2] Preliminary findings indicate that if women enter the labour market they continue to work, though they may take 4–5 year breaks after marriage or pregnancy.

[3] Sen delivered this lecture at the Economics Department, University of Calcutta.

realise that an action like shifting to a nuclear family has its costs as multi-generational bonds would weaken. Similarly, Priyanka asserts that her decision to stay with her family is due to emotional attachments, and not compulsion. As a result, in many cases, the outcome is not apparently different from the outcome under patriarchy to a substantial extent. There is, however, one major difference—the outcome is the result of an exercise in the autonomy and agency of the women. The freedom to choose between outcomes, we argue, is the most important effect of employment in the IT sector on women's empowerment.

References

Banerjee, N. (1985). *Women workers in the unorganized sector: The Calcutta experience.* Hyderabad: Sangam Books Pvt Ltd.

Banerjee, N. (1991). *Indian women in a changing industrial scenario.* New Delhi: Sage Publishers.

Banerjee, N. (1992). Poverty, work and gender in urban India. Occasional Papers No. 133, Centre for Studies in Social Sciences, Kolkata.

Drew, E., Humphreys, P.C., & Murphy, C. (2003). *Off The Treadmill: Achieving Work/Life Balance.* National Framework Committee for Family Friendly Policies: Dublin.

Elson, D., & Pearson, R. (1981). Nimble fingers make cheap workers: An analysis of women's employment in Third World export manufacturing. *Feminist Review, Spring, 7,* 87–107.

Harriss, B. (1995). The intra-family distribution of hunger in South Asia. In J. Drèze, A.K. Sen and A. Hussain (Ed.) *The political economy of hunger: Selected essays.* Clarendon Press: Oxford: 224–297.

Kenny, M. (1978). *Woman X two: How to cope with a double life.* Hamlyn: Middlesex.

Lim, L. Y. C. (1990). Women's work in export factories: The politics of a cause. In Irene Tinker (Ed.), *Persistent inequalities: Women and world development* (pp. 101–119). Oxford: Oxford University Press.

Mies, M. (1986). *Patriarchy and accumulation on a world scale.* London: Zed Press.

Mukhopadhyay, C. C., & Seymour, S. (1994). Introduction and theoetical overview. In C. C. Mukhopadhyay & S. Seymour (Eds.), *Women, education and family structure in India* (pp. 1–33). Boulder: Westview Press.

Noronha, E., & D'Cruz, P. (2008). The dynamics of teleworking. *Gender, Technology and Development, 12*(2), 157–183.

Proctor, I., & Padefield, M. (1998). *Young adult women, work and family: Living a contradiction.* London: Mansell.

Redmond, J., Valiulis, M., & Drew, E. (2006). *Literature review of issues related to work-life balance, workplace culture and maternity/childcare issues.* Report No. 16, Crisis Pregnancy Agency: Dublin. Accessed at http://bit.ly/J5KAq1 on 12 March 2013.

Walby, S. (1997). *Gender transformations.* London: Routledge.

Young, M., & Willmott, P. (1973). *The symmetrical family.* London: Routledge & Kegan Paul.

Appendix A

(See Tables A.1 and A.2).

Table A.1 Trends in LFPR by gender and difference: 1990–2010

Year	South Asia			World		
	Female	Male	Difference	Female	Male	Difference
1990	35.7	85.3	49.6	52.1	80.6	28.5
1991	36.0	85.0	49.0	52.3	80.5	28.2
1992	36.1	84.8	48.7	52.4	80.3	27.9
1993	36.2	84.5	48.3	52.2	80.0	27.8
1994	36.4	84.3	48.0	52.3	79.8	27.5
1995	35.9	84.1	48.2	52.2	79.6	27.4
1996	35.8	84.0	48.2	52.1	79.4	27.3
1997	35.6	83.8	48.3	52.1	79.2	27.1
1998	35.5	83.6	48.1	52.0	78.9	26.9
1999	35.1	83.5	48.3	52.1	78.9	26.7
2000	34.9	83.3	48.4	52.0	78.6	26.6
2001	35.3	83.3	47.9	52.0	78.4	26.4
2002	35.8	83.3	47.5	52.1	78.2	26.1
2003	36.3	83.4	47.1	52.2	78.1	25.9
2004	36.7	83.3	46.6	52.3	78.0	25.8
2005	37.4	83.5	46.1	52.4	78.0	25.6
2006	36.3	83.1	46.8	52.2	77.9	25.7
2007	35.0	82.6	47.6	52.0	77.7	25.7
2008	33.9	82.1	48.2	51.7	77.6	25.9
2009	32.8	81.7	48.9	51.4	77.3	25.9
2010	31.7	81.3	49.6	51.2	77.2	26.0

Source World Development Indicators data set: Accessed from http://bit.ly/phxEiy on 20 October 2012

Z. Husain and M. Dutta, *Women in Kolkata's IT Sector*,
SpringerBriefs in Sociology, DOI: 10.1007/978-81-322-1593-6,
© The Author(s) 2014

Table A.2 Difference in LFPR across gender, by regions (percentage points)

Year	East Asia and Pacific	Europe and Central Asia	Latin America and Caribbean	Middle East and North Africa	South Asia	Sub-Saharan Africa
1990	5.1	32.7	36.2	57.2	49.6	21.2
1991	4.8	32.6	34.5	57.2	49.0	20.6
1992	4.0	33.3	31.9	56.9	48.7	19.9
1993	3.2	34.1	31.9	56.6	48.3	19.3
1994	2.6	34.2	31.2	55.8	48.0	18.8
1995	2.3	33.9	29.8	55.7	48.2	18.3
1996	2.0	33.3	29.5	55.7	48.2	17.9
1997	1.8	33.8	27.8	55.6	48.3	17.4
1998	1.7	33.8	26.9	55.4	48.1	16.8
1999	2.2	32.5	26.2	54.9	48.3	16.3
2000	2.1	32.1	26.0	54.7	48.4	15.7
2001	1.7	32.1	24.8	54.4	47.9	15.0
2002	1.7	31.7	23.8	54.1	47.5	14.4
2003	1.7	31.4	23.8	52.9	47.1	13.8
2004	2.0	31.6	23.1	52.2	46.6	13.3
2005	2.5	31.3	22.8	51.7	46.1	13.3
2006	2.7	30.8	21.9	51.9	46.8	13.2
2007	3.0	30.3	21.5	51.4	47.6	13.2
2008	3.6	30.2	20.8	51.5	48.2	13.2
2009	3.7	29.6	20.5	50.4	48.9	13.1
2010	3.6	29.6	20.1	49.4	49.6	13.1

Source World Development Indicators data set: Accessed from http://bit.ly/phxEiy on 20 October 2012

Appendix B
Media Reportings About IT Sector

The Economic Times, "Psychiatrists report sudden rise in cases of depression among IT workers, Nasscom says all is well", 25 April 2013. Accessed at http://bit.ly/15XK4mv, on 23 July 2013.

Times of India, "BPO blues", 10 October 2010. Accessed at http://bit.ly/163PDMT, on 23 July 2013.

Andrew Marantz, "My summer at an Indian Call Centre", Accessed at http://bit.ly/jAK6aF, on 23 July 2013.

Times of India, "Depressed call centre employee commits suicide", 14 February, 2013. Accessed at http://bit.ly/161Bvp, 23 July 2013.

Times of India, "Murder of call centre employee shocks Bangalore", 17 December, 2005. Accessed at http://bit.ly/139Di7x, 23 July 2013.

India Today, "Call centre employee found murdered in Noida, police suspect she was raped", 5 January, 2013. Accessed at http://bit.ly/UpUVvY, 23 July 2013.

Times of India, "Girl jumps to death", 12 December 2007, Accessed at http://bit.ly/1bIHe7R, on 23 July 2013.

Kolkata on wheels, "Drugs: City on a high". Accessed at http://bit.ly/13zW4bH, on 23 July 2013.

Z. Husain and M. Dutta, *Women in Kolkata's IT Sector*,
SpringerBriefs in Sociology, DOI: 10.1007/978-81-322-1593-6,
© The Author(s) 2014